VEG EVERYTHING

RECIPES FOR WEEKNIGHTS, PARTIES AND THE BITES IN BETWEEN

The New York Times

Cooking

TEN SPEED PRESS
California | New York

TANYA SICHYNSKY
VEG
EVERYTHING

CONTENTS

INTRODUCTION 6
HOW TO USE THIS BOOK 10
NEED HELP DECIDING? 12
MEET THE CONTRIBUTORS 14

1 EARLY BIRD SPECIALS 18
START YOUR DAY THE VEGETABLE WAY

2 SALAD DAYS 46
GENRE-BENDING BOUNTIES FOR EVERY SEASON

3 PLATE OPTIONAL 76
WRAPS, SANDWICHES AND OTHER HANDY CLASSICS FOR EASY EATING

4 SOUP WEATHER 104
BROTHY, CREAMY, CHUNKY VEHICLES FOR MARKET HAULS AND REFRIGERATOR SCRAPS

5 **MEATLESS MONDAYS** 136
GO-TO WEEKNIGHT DINNERS THAT MAKE THE MOST OF TOFU, MUSHROOMS AND MORE

6 **NEW COMFORTS** 160
COZY MEALS THAT PROVE THE POWER OF A WELL-STOCKED PANTRY

7 **RSVP-WORTHY** 190
VEGETABLE HEADLINERS TO WOW YOUR GUESTS

8 **VEG ESSENTIALS** 222
FOUNDATIONAL RECIPES TO GET YOU STARTED

ACKNOWLEDGMENTS 236

INDEX 237

INTRODUCTION

Let's get one thing out of the way. I'm not a vegetarian.

No, no! Don't go anywhere. If you're looking for labels, I can give you a few. I'm Tanya, an editor for Cooking and Food at *The New York Times.* I'm a Leo (Aries rising, Libra moon). I'm an omnivore, yes. And I'm also a vegetable devotee and the keyboard warrior behind *The Veggie,* the *Times's* weekly newsletter dedicated to exuberant meatless cooking.

When we set out to create *The Veggie,* I learned a couple things: A majority of our readers weren't vegetarian either, but many wanted to up their daily vegetable intake, and more than a few had no idea where to begin. They'd ask questions I had bashfully reserved for Google not all that long ago: What can I eat for a vegetable-based breakfast? How do I anchor a dinner party or holiday table? Can I make this meaty dish . . . without the meat? Will I feel full? If you've asked any of these questions, boy, do I have the book for you.

This is the sort of book I could've used a few years back.

I liked vegetables plenty growing up—my parents never had to land a broccoli airplane on my tongue tarmac. But on my childhood dinner table, they were the slight curves that made up a well-rounded meal, all bending around a meaty centerpiece that required more thought, more preparation, more labor. A platter draped in thin slices of tomato and milky cheese drizzled with balsamic vinegar and dusted with freshly cracked black pepper could amount to "a vegetable." Garden-style salads with crisp romaine, thick-cut cucumbers and a bridal shop of assorted dressings, just say yes, made near-nightly appearances. Tomato, avocado and red onion salads and platanos maduros were a given in our Cuban-Ukrainian-American home. So were French fries—Dad's favorite—retrieved from the oil just as we sat to stave off a reality as morose as death and taxes: a cold, languid fry. In the spring, there were thick spears of grilled asparagus, and in the summer, hearty planks of zucchini and ears of sweet corn, all branded by the grill. I piled my plate with them all.

Depending on where and when you grew up, a meat-and-three style of eating might sound familiar to you, too. For the better part of my life, this was the only way I knew how to eat or cook.

After college, I took part in the disorienting tradition of moving to a new city. I settled into

> **“THE DECISION TO EAT MORE VEGETABLES DOES NOT CONFINE YOU TO A LIFE OF SIDE DISHES. QUITE THE OPPOSITE. IT OPENS THE DOOR TO A MULTIVERSE.”**

the smallest room in a house with six roommates (two bathrooms, one fridge and at least one dead rat in the pantry). I worked nights and weekends, which wasn't great for the ol' social life. To pass the afternoons, I'd pop on a podcast and amble around town, my only destination being a specialty grocer or a sprawling farmers' market some internet list insisted I visit.

There I found bundles of gangly carrots, their spindly roots intertwined like shoelaces. Crates of eggplants in shades I'd never seen before. Oyster mushrooms overflowing from paper bags. Bunches of herbs that could double as bridal bouquets. Rows and rows of bulbous, beautiful tomatoes. Wax beans that, from a stall away, looked a lot like French fries.

Moved by their glamour and my own curiosity, I'd buy one or two of whatever looked best and furiously Google things like "spikey spiral neon green cauliflower what is it" on the walk home. (I imagine my initial encounter with romanesco mimicked man's first impression of an octopus. Alien? God?) But what to do with them?

I loved to cook, even in my seven-person kitchen, and I wasn't half bad at it. Food magazines, Instagram and the sporadic restaurant visit, meanwhile, were making a compelling case for putting vegetables smack-dab in the middle of the plate. (Although the appeals of a meatless meal were plenty, one stood out: I wasn't exactly swimming in cash. See the six roommates.)

I knew my market jewels deserved more. I wanted to experience every flavor and texture they could offer, not shroud them in the shadow of some chop or steak.

Change happened incrementally. There were many veg-heavy (but not entirely meatless) pastas, like a sorta pasta alla norma that I thought needed pancetta (it didn't). There was the Great Sweet Potato Fixation: soups, hashes, mashes, chips, fries, you name it. At one point, I got really into turning cauliflower into pizza crust. Look, it was 2015.

Those first forays into more vegetable-forward cooking felt a little like Jenga. When I tugged at what I thought was a foundational block—the meat—to my surprise, the tower stood firm. I made dreamy chickpea stews and tried my hand at swapping tofu into saag paneer. I wowed friends with stunning tomato and ricotta tarts and melon and avocado salads. Over time, my cravings for vegetables only intensified. Their absence from meals became a glaring omission, not a careless

oversight. "Where are the greens?" I'd plead to one particularly meat-devoted boyfriend. Like so many other home cooks, my palate has lurched toward plants for reasons of health, environment and taste. And I've become a sharper, more creative, more thoughtful cook for it.

There are as many reasons to eat more vegetables as there are varieties. But I'm not your doctor nor your mommy. I'm not here to be prescriptive. My only goal is to help you harness vegetables' (okay, and fruits') deliciousness at every turn and meal, for every mood and season. Whether you're a decadeslong vegetarian or a casual observer of Meatless Monday, a climate-conscious eater or you just really love vegetables, damn it, this cookbook has 100 ways to do so.

In the end, speaking meat-and-three with native fluency has helped me meet readers—who you'll see recipe comments from throughout this book—wherever they are. Even if you're only a little vegetable-curious. Even if you need just one place to start. The 100 vegetarian recipes in this book are crafted by some of the greatest minds in the game, developers devoted to vegetarian cooking, like Hetty Lui McKinnon, as well as omnivores with uniquely playful approaches to vegetables, like Alexa Weibel, paving the way for an evening or a lifetime of vegging any and everything. Start your stroll wherever you see fit; there is no wrong way in. And there are lessons and tricks tucked into each introduction and every recipe, courtesy of the talented recipe developers I call colleagues and teachers.

Transformative tofu techniques, oomph-packed dressings, a powerhouse on pantry staples—these are the true load-bearing Jenga blocks that helped me shift the center of my tower's gravity and champion vegetables, rather than cast them to the side. Finish this book having retained even one recipe from our Veg Essentials chapter, like **VEGETABLE STOCK** (page 224) or a **BIG POT OF BEANS** (page 227) or a **MISO-SESAME VINAIGRETTE THAT'S GOOD ON ANYTHING** (page 232), and I promise you'll be able to veg at least a few things. That is my money-back guarantee. (My publisher says that's not how books work. Alas.)

The most important takeaway? That the decision to eat more vegetables does not confine you to a lifetime of side dishes. Quite the opposite. It opens the door to a multiverse where infinite versions of main-course salads test and warp what you thought a salad could be; where meaty mushrooms shine in crispy tacos, on the grill and tucked into luxurious puff pastry; where eggplant, greens and chickpeas are treated with the same reverence as a Rockwellian meaty main; and where you can veg everything and eat better for it.

HOW TO USE THIS BOOK

The pages ahead are bursting with tips and tricks to enhance your veg-forward cooking. Some of you may not need a manual for this book. Just put it in drive and be on your way to the next delicious destination! But for those newer to meatless cooking, or for those looking to expand their vegetable knowledge, allow the following principles to be your guide. You don't need any fancy gadgets to cook from this book—just a can-do attitude, a willingness to read the recipes in their entirety before you start the car, and an appetite.

THINK SEASONALLY

Big Grocery Store means you can access many of the vegetables featured here year-round. But a tomato in February just doesn't quite hit. That's why in the Need Help Deciding? section, I've outlined a handful of recipes perfect for each season. When it comes to expanding your vegetable repertoire, eat produce at its best and you will always be set up for success.

Beyond those suggestions, feel empowered to make season-based swaps. A recipe that features raw vegetables or takes a low-intervention approach, like blanching, blistering or sautéing, may not shine as bright when prepared with out-of-season produce, which can taste dull, watery or woody.

Peak-season vegetables will always be sweeter, snappier and juicier, significantly improving your effort-to-reward ratio.

In Lemony Orzo with Asparagus and Garlic Bread Crumbs on page 172, for example, try swapping in broccoli in the fall and zucchini in the summer; in the More-Vegetable-Than-Egg Frittata on page 36, try a combination of sliced potatoes, kale and grated carrot in the cooler months and baby spinach, peas and asparagus as soon as the weather warms.

KNOW THY TOFU

The recipes in this book call for one of three kinds of block tofu: silken, firm or extra-firm. Blocks tend to come in 14-or 16-ounce packages. Some recipes work well with either size, while others might specify one weight for proportion purposes.

Silken tofu is not pressed, so its high water content means it's jiggly and soft, like custard. It is delicate, so slice with care. It can be eaten chilled with little more than a simple dressing but is especially lovely scooped into soups or salads. Firm tofu is always worth throwing in the grocery cart, as it's the most versatile packaged option. It's absorbent and plush but also crisps up nicely. Extra-firm tofu is dense and compact and typically has the lowest water content. It retains its shape even when jostled around in stir-fries and stews and is ideal for crumbling and grating.

Some flexible recipes will call for either firm or extra-firm tofu; in those cases, use what's available to you knowing the results won't differ much.

And while a tofu press can be helpful for extracting moisture, I'll tell you right now: You don't need one. To prepare firm or extra-firm tofu for optimal crisping, simply wrap it in paper towels or a clean dish towel and set a large skillet or a sheet pan holding something heavy, like canned beans, on top. You want to expel the liquid gently so that the tofu doesn't break and crumble.

CHECK THE LABEL

Parmesan, a rich source of umami, appears in recipes throughout this book. Many cheeses are considered ovo-lacto-vegetarian-friendly, meaning they're safe for those who do not eat meat or fish but do eat animal by-products like dairy and eggs. Parmigiano-Reggiano, however, contains animal rennet—enzymes derived from the stomachs of calves and other ruminants—as do some other hard cheeses, like certain Cheddars.

Depending on your dietary needs or restrictions, you may want to seek out Parmesan expressly labeled "vegetarian," which will use nonanimal rennet derived from vegetables or fungi. You can double-check the product's ingredient list to see if "vegetarian enzymes," "vegetable enzymes" or "microbial enzymes" appear, or ask your cheesemonger for help. For vegan alternatives, seek out dairy-free Parmesan-style cheeses, or, depending on the recipe, use nutritional yeast in Parm's place.

You will also see a handful of recipes that call for red or green curry paste, a stellar staple for building big flavor with little effort. Some varieties of curry paste may contain dried shrimp or fish sauce, though seafood-free products, such as those from the popular brand Thai Kitchen, are readily available at major grocery stores.

If you're not sure, simply read the back of the jar.

SPEAKING OF SWAPS

One of the many beauties of cooking is figuring out what works for you, and I encourage you to experiment with what you have on hand. But you also don't want to waste your dinner on a bad ingredient swap.

Alliums (onions, shallots, scallions) are, for the most part, interchangeable. Your dish won't be ruined if you swap red onions for shallots or scallions for white onions. Other vegetable swaps are dependent largely on use, so consider flavor, density, texture and how quickly something cooks. If a recipe calls for, say, Swiss chard, you can substitute a similarly hearty green, like kale or escarole. Many dishes in this book include vegetable swap options in the note that precedes the recipe or in the ingredient list. Still, many substitutions can be subjective. If you don't like cilantro, don't force it. You have my permission to use parsley (or another tender herb like basil, chives or mint).

Oils and fats are easy swaps, but be mindful of flavor and the smoke point, the temperature at which they begin to burn. Butter has a low smoke point; avocado oil, refined sesame oil and olive oil have a medium-high smoke point; and canola oil, coconut oil and vegetable oil have a high smoke point.

HOW TO USE THIS BOOK

Finally, note that honey is not vegan, so if you need to veganize a dish, try an equal amount of vegan pure maple syrup (check the label) or brown sugar if needed.

AUDIT YOUR PANTRY

Throughout the 100 recipes ahead, you'll see a handful of pantry staples make repeat appearances for their ability to infuse a dish with deep savoriness. Ingredients like tomato paste, soy sauce, white miso paste, canned coconut milk, chile crisp and nut butters (like cashew, almond and peanut) really get their reps in, and they're worth having on hand for regular exuberant meatless cooking. You may see staples like canned chipotles in adobo, dried mushrooms and nutritional yeast less frequently, but they are just as capable of lifting a dish to flavorful new heights and have long shelf lives, so give them a go if they're not already on your grocery list.

Canned beans are economical, so stock up. Many of the recipes in this book, including the popular recipe for Creamy, Spicy Tomato Beans and Greens on the opposite page, call for them because of their accessibility. But if your grocery store has a great dried beans setup or you're in a bean club, do cook a Big Pot of Beans (page 227). One standard 15-ounce can of black beans, white beans or chickpeas is equivalent to roughly 1½ cups, and you can easily swap your from-scratch beans in any recipe that calls for canned.

CONSIDER THE SALT

You'll see a few different salts mentioned throughout this book. If a recipe simply calls for "salt," you can use whatever you have on hand; the recipe will ask you to season to your tastes as you go. A recipe that calls for "kosher salt, such as Diamond Crystal," was tested with Diamond Crystal kosher salt, which is less salty than other salts by volume. Similarly, anything that calls for "coarse kosher salt" was tested with Morton's coarse kosher salt—use that. And when you see a measured amount of "fine sea salt," use whatever brand of fine table salt you have.

It's important to adhere to the recipe, as the salinity will vary by brand. For example, 1 tablespoon of Diamond Crystal salt is equal to 10 grams, while 1 tablespoon of table salt is almost double the weight, at 19 grams.

A NOTE ON VEGAN RECIPES

We've got you covered. While there are plenty of easy swaps to make many of these vegetarian recipes vegan (check Need Help Deciding? on page 14 and read the notes at the beginning of recipes for additional guidance), more than half of this book is already suitable for a vegan diet. Fifty-one recipes, in fact! You can easily find them by the icon on the recipe pages or in the index under "vegan." (Some of these labeled recipes include ingredient options to make them vegan, such as oil as an alternative for butter, and others may note non-vegan ingredients as optional.)

AND A WORD ON FRUITS

Lastly, I know tomatoes (and eggplant and zucchini and cucumbers and so on) are technically fruit. Please, just humor me.

NEED HELP DECIDING?

VEGAN MASTERPIECES

Look for the green VEGAN tag for all 51 vegan recipes.

57 Vegan Caesar Salad with Crisp Chickpeas

100 Vegan al Pastor Tacos

171 Vegan Cacio e Pepe

219 Vegan Salted Maple Ginger Pie

233 Vegan Green Goddess Dressing

EAT THIS IN THE FALL

54 Brown Butter Lentil and Sweet Potato Salad

114 Lemony Carrot and Cauliflower Soup

124 Butternut Squash and Green Curry Soup

151 White Beans au Vin

168 Carrot Risotto with Chile Crisp

187 Crisp Gnocchi with Brussels Sprouts and Brown Butter

210 Whole Roasted Squash with Tomato-Ginger Chickpeas

EAT THIS IN THE WINTER

70 Roasted Vegetables with Creamy Coconut Dressing

106 Creamy Cauliflower Soup with Rosemary Olive Oil

110 Cabbage and Parmesan Soup

165 Brown Butter Bucatini with Charred Cabbage

175 Porcini Ragù

184 Cheesy Cabbage Tteokbokki

196 Mushroom Bourguignon

EAT THIS IN THE SPRING

51 Extra-Green Pasta Salad

123 Spring Minestrone with Kale and Pasta

172 Lemony Orzo with Asparagus and Garlic Bread Crumbs

179 Crispy Rice with Dill and Runny Eggs

204 Kuku Sabzi (Herb and Scallion Frittata)

216 White Lasagna

EAT THIS IN THE SUMMER

48 Dumpling Tomato Salad with Chile Crisp Vinaigrette

61 Cold Tofu Salad with Tomatoes and Peaches

62 Miso Eggplant Salad with Chickpeas

66 Chopped Salad with Jalapeño-Ranch Dressing

73 Spicy Cucumbers with Yogurt, Lemon and Herbs

96 Grilled Mushroom Skewers in Red Chile Paste

99 Pimento Cheese and Tomato Sandwiches

FOR THE VEGETABLE-AVERSE KID (OR ADULT)

Kid-tested and approved.

81 Roasted Vegetable Burritos

82 Indian-ish Nachos with Cheddar, Black Beans and Chutney

86 Crispy Mushroom Tacos

131 Coconut Black Bean Soup

154 Sweet and Sour Cauliflower

162 Creamy, Spicy Tomato Beans and Greens

172 Lemony Orzo with Asparagus and Garlic Bread Crumbs

187 Crisp Gnocchi with Brussels Sprouts and Brown Butter

I CAN'T BELIEVE IT'S NOT MAGIC

Six meals with 6 ingredients or fewer (not including salt, pepper, oil and optional ingredients).

35 Tofu Scramble

36 More-Vegetable-Than-Egg Frittata

45 Everyday Dal

142 Cabbage Parm

188 Silken Tofu with Spicy Soy Dressing

209 Borani Banjan (Afghan-style Eggplant in Yogurt)

PACK IT UP

Vegetables that can go where you go.

27 Green Smoothie

38 Make-Ahead Egg, Spinach and Feta Wraps

65 Corn and Miso Pasta Salad

69 Quinoa and Broccoli Spoon Salad

74 Orzo Salad with Lentils and Zucchini

85 Crunchy Veggie Wraps with Kabocha Squash

90 Cauliflower Salad Sandwiches

93 Chickpea Salad Sandwiches

OH BABY, I *LOVE* THIS SONG

These recipes have gone triple platinum in my home.

51 Extra-Green Pasta Salad

61 Cold Tofu Salad with Tomatoes and Peaches

78 Cauliflower Shawarma with Spicy Tahini

86 Crispy Mushroom Tacos

109 Golden Potato and Greens Soup

147 Portobello au Poivre

148 Coconut Saag

157 Mushroom Laab

200 Dumplings with Chile Crisp

MORE BEANS!

Fiber and protein in one tiny package.

20 Huevos Enfrijolados (Eggs in Spicy Black Beans)

52 No-Cook Chili Bean Salad

94 Buffalo White Beans

120 Gochujang Potato Stew

127 White Bean, Rice and Dill Soup

141 Chickpea Picadillo

152 Vegetarian Tamale Pie

176 Chana Masala

180 Vegetarian Skillet Chili

183 Coconut Curry Chickpeas with Pumpkin and Lime

PIE BY ANY OTHER NAME

Would taste as delicious!

58 Salad Pizza with White Beans and Parmesan

198 Creamed Greens Potpie

202 Chickpea, Spinach and Feta Pie

212 Vegetarian Shepherd's Pie

214 Asparagus, Goat Cheese and Tarragon Tart

219 Vegan Salted Maple Ginger Pie

OOPS, NO VEGGIES

171 Vegan Cacio e Pepe

ARE THERE SWEETS IN THIS BOOK?

Well, yes.

32 Zucchini Muffins with Cinnamon Crunch Topping

41 Lemon Ricotta Pancakes

219 Vegan Salted Maple Ginger Pie

MEET THE CONTRIBUTORS

YOSSY AREFI is a Brooklyn-based recipe developer, photographer and food stylist. She is the author of *Snacking Bakes* and *Snacking Cakes.*

HANA ASBRINK is currently the deputy food editor of *Bon Appétit* and *Epicurious.* As a journalist, recipe developer and podcast host, she has contributed to NYT Cooking, Food52, Chowhound, Bloomberg Television, and more.

ANDY BARAGHANI is a cook, food writer and the James Beard Award–winning author of *The Cook You Want to Be.*

MARK BITTMAN is the author of the How to Cook Everything series and *Animal, Vegetable, Junk.* After three decades at *The New York Times,* he is now editor in chief of *The Bittman Project* and the founder of Community Kitchen.

KAY CHUN is a chef, recipe developer and regular contributor to NYT Cooking. She is the author of the cookbook *Gather Around My Table*. She has been a writer and editor at several food publications, including *Food & Wine, Bon Appétit, Gourmet* and *Real Simple.*

MELISSA CLARK is a food reporter and columnist for *The New York Times* and NYT Cooking, for which she creates recipes, hosts videos and is one of the writers of the Cooking newsletter. She's also written dozens of cookbooks, most recently *Dinner in One.*

SARAH COPELAND is the bestselling author of *Feast, Every Day Is Saturday* and *Instant Family Meals.* An alum of *Real Simple, Food & Wine,* and the former host of Food Network series "Every Day Is Saturday," she is the creator of Edible Living and pens a Substack newsletter by the same name.

KIA DAMON is a chef and recipe developer residing in the South. Her work is featured in NYT Cooking, *Southern Living,* Food52, and The Kitchn. Her forthcoming debut cookbook highlights Florida's rich culinary contributions.

NAZ DERAVIAN is a Los Angeles–based writer. She is the award-winning author of the cookbook *Bottom of the Pot: Persian Recipes and Stories.*

SARAH DIGREGORIO is a critically acclaimed journalist. Her work has appeared in major national publications, and she is the author of two reported nonfiction books and one cookbook.

HAM EL-WAYLLY is a chef, recipe developer and video creator based in New York City. He is the author of *Hello, Home Cooking* and the chef/partner of the restaurant Strange Delight in Brooklyn, New York.

SOHLA EL-WAYLLY is a food writer, recipe developer and video host. She's been featured on HBO Max, History Channel and the NYT Cooking and *Bon Appétit* YouTube channels, and is the author of the James Beard Award–winning cookbook *Start Here.*

KRISTINA FELIX is a recipe developer and tester for NYT Cooking and is the author of a forthcoming cookbook on Mexican soups and stews from Workman Publishing to be published in 2027.

JERRELLE GUY is a food writer, photographer and contributor to NYT Cooking based in Dallas. She is the author of cookbooks *Black Girl Baking* and *We Fancy,* and the newsletter "The Dinner Ritual."

LIDEY HEUCK is a cook, writer, contributor to NYT Cooking and the author of *Cooking in Real Life.*

BECKY HUGHES is the social media editor for NYT Cooking, where she also cowrites the "Where to Eat: New York City" newsletter.

ERIC KIM is a food columnist for *The New York Times* and a recipe developer and video host for NYT Cooking. A native of Atlanta, he is the author of the cookbook *Korean American.*

GENEVIEVE KO is a senior editor for NYT Cooking and Food at *The New York Times,* where she also writes a column, develops recipes and appears in videos. In addition to writing her own cookbook, *Better Baking,* she has contributed to more than twenty cookbooks.

YEWANDE KOMOLAFE is a cooking writer and columnist for *The New York Times* and a recipe developer and video host for NYT Cooking. She is the author of the cookbook *My Everyday Lagos.*

PRIYA KRISHNA is a food reporter for *The New York Times* and video host of the NYT Cooking YouTube series *On the Job,* spotlighting the vital and often unseen labor in the food industry. She is the bestselling author of multiple cookbooks, including *Indian-ish,* and her stories have been included in *The Best American Food Writing* and nominated for a James Beard and IACP Award. She is originally from Dallas, Texas.

SUE LI is a food stylist and recipe developer, and frequent contributor to NYT Cooking. She previously worked at *Bon Appétit.*

J. KENJI LÓPEZ-ALT is a contributor to *The New York Times* and NYT Cooking. He is also the author of *The Food Lab* and *The Wok,* the creator and host of *Kenji's Cooking Show* on YouTube and co-creator of the podcast *The Recipe with Kenji and Deb.*

RICK A. MARTÍNEZ is a Mexican American recipe developer, food personality, NYT Cooking contributor and author of the cookbooks *Mi Cocina* and *Salsa Daddy.*

HETTY LUI MCKINNON is a cook, food writer and regular contributor to *The New York Times.* She is the author of *Linger, Tenderheart* and four other cookbooks.

LIGAYA MISHAN is the co-chief restaurant critic for *The New York Times.* She has written for the *New York Review of Books* and *The New Yorker,* and her work has appeared in the Best American anthologies in Magazine, Food and Travel Writing.

SAMIN NOSRAT is a cook, teacher and author of the cookbook *Good Things* and the James Beard Award–winning *Salt, Fat, Acid, Heat.* She is the co-host (with Hrishikesh Hirway) of the *Home Cooking* podcast, a former Eat columnist at *The New York Times Magazine* and the host of the Netflix original documentary series based on her book *Salt, Fat, Acid, Heat.*

SHEELA PRAKASH is a food writer, recipe developer and the author of three cookbooks, *Salad Seasons, Mediterranean Every Day* and the soon to be published *Spaghettata.*

JOCELYN RAMIREZ is a chef, the author of the cookbook *La Vida Verde* and a *New York Times* recipe contributor. She is also a yogi and entrepreneur committed to creating more accessibility to true-to-culture products and recipes for her community.

SAMANTHA SENEVIRATNE is a baker, food stylist, recipe developer, NYT Cooking contributor, television personality and the author of four cookbooks, most recently *Bake Smart.*

ZAINAB SHAH is a contributor to NYT Cooking and the vice president of audience strategy at the American Journalism Project.

TANYA SICHYNSKY is a Food and Cooking editor for *The New York Times* and the host and author of *The Veggie,* a YouTube series and weekly vegetarian newsletter.

ALI SLAGLE is a recipe developer who specializes in low-effort, high-reward recipes. She is the author of the cookbook *I Dream of Dinner (So You Don't Have To).* Her next cookbook, on plants, will be published in 2027.

ALEXA WEIBEL is a senior staff editor and recipe developer at NYT Cooking. She was previously an editor at *Every Day with Rachael Ray* magazine, a cookbook editor and a restaurant line cook.

CHAPTER 1

EARLY BIRD SPECIALS

Amid a whirl of meetings or responsibilities, sometimes lunch evades us, and dinner is a quick slice of pizza on the commute home, less balanced than we intended. By tucking some greens into breakfast, you'll never crawl into bed that night wondering: Wait, did I eat a vegetable today? Big Productivity maintains that the most efficient way to establish new routines is to habit stack: By connecting one new habit to an established one, you're more likely to remember and maintain it. That's why, if your goal is to eat more vegetables, you should stack them onto breakfast, the first—and so-called most important—meal of the day.

It worked for me. I've never been great at routines, but on my most hectic days, I'm grateful for the version of myself who sleep-walks into the kitchen and ensures I start my day with something more energizing than two iced lattes and a packet of gummy vitamins. That something is often green juice, which really is no more virtuous than a banana or a bowl of yogurt, but boy does it make me feel like I'm doing *something* right.

Spinach and ginger are nonnegotiable, and they shine in Ali Slagle's refreshing and wholesome Green Smoothie (page 27). Even half asleep, you too can throw a few ingredients into a blender and let it rip. It's the perfect companion to Ali's Tofu Scramble (page 35), which is so good that I set my alarm 15 minutes earlier to guarantee I have enough time to make it. If protein is a priority, her recipe is a flavorful plant-based alternative to eggs—one that that you can add even more vegetables to, you overachiever.

Or keep the eggs, and surround them with your favorite greens or beans, as in Sarah Copeland's Green Shakshuka with Avocado and Lime (page 31) or Rick Martínez's Huevos Enfrijolados (Eggs in Spicy Black Beans, page 20). Throughout this chapter, there are breakfasts to rush out of the house with and others to linger over, all in service of moving you in whatever direction the day demands—even if that direction is Lemon Ricotta Pancakes (page 41). We can count homemade blueberry syrup as a vegetable this one time. These aren't just breakfasts worth getting up for. These are breakfasts worth building an entire morning routine around. And if you're still not convinced, many of these recipes double as weeknight dinners for my committed night owls.

HUEVOS ENFRIJOLADOS (EGGS IN SPICY BLACK BEANS)
PAGE 20

SWEET POTATO HASH WITH TOFU
PAGE 23

BREAKFAST UDON
PAGE 24

GREEN SMOOTHIE
PAGE 27

GOAT CHEESE AND DILL DUTCH BABY
PAGE 28

GREEN SHAKSHUKA WITH AVOCADO AND LIME
PAGE 31

ZUCCHINI MUFFINS WITH CINNAMON CRUNCH TOPPING
PAGE 32

TOFU SCRAMBLE
PAGE 35

MORE-VEGETABLE-THAN-EGG FRITTATA
PAGE 36

MAKE-AHEAD EGG, SPINACH AND FETA WRAPS
PAGE 38

LEMON RICOTTA PANCAKES
PAGE 41

CHEESY POTATO BREAKFAST TACOS
PAGE 42

EVERYDAY DAL
PAGE 45

HUEVOS ENFRIJOLADOS (EGGS IN SPICY BLACK BEANS)

time 40 minutes

yield 4 servings

Eggs nestled in a spicy, smoky black bean sauce are a staple of Mexican home cooking. It's a quick way to make a meal from what's already in the kitchen: leftover frijoles de olla, chiles and fresh eggs. In this version, canned black beans are cooked with chipotles and garlic until rich and creamy, then eggs are gently dropped into the simmering beans to poach. Served with crunchy tostadas, queso fresco and avocado, it's a deeply comforting, pantry-friendly meal that comes together in under 45 minutes—perfect for a quick and hearty brunch or a weeknight dinner.

—Rick A. Martínez

3 tablespoons vegetable oil

½ cup chopped white onion

3 garlic cloves, crushed

3 to 5 canned chipotle chiles in adobo (to taste), chopped, plus 2 tablespoons adobo sauce

2 (15-ounce) cans black beans, rinsed and drained

1¼ cups vegetable or mushroom broth

Salt

6 to 8 large eggs

3 ounces queso fresco or Cotija cheese, crumbled

Cilantro leaves with tender stems and sliced avocado, for serving

8 corn tostadas

1. In a large skillet with a lid, heat the oil over medium and add ¼ cup onion, the garlic and chopped chipotles. Cook, stirring occasionally, until tender and beginning to brown, 6 to 8 minutes. Add the beans, adobo sauce and broth and bring to a boil. Cook, stirring occasionally, until the liquid has reduced slightly, about 5 minutes. Off the heat, use a potato masher to smash the beans until no whole beans remain. Taste and season with salt.
2. Return the pan to medium-high heat. Use a spoon to make wells in the beans, gently crack the eggs into the simmering bean mixture and season each with salt. Reduce heat to medium and cook until the eggs are just set, 5 to 7 minutes. If you prefer hard-cooked eggs, cover the skillet and cook for 8 to 10 minutes.
3. Top huevos enfrijolados with the queso, cilantro and remaining ¼ cup chopped onion and serve with sliced avocado and tostadas alongside.

"Adobo chile hack—we buy 2 to 3 cans and then just purée with an immersion blender and freeze in ice cube trays (when frozen, put cubes in a pickle jar for storing)."

—Beth H

"Simple, delicious, accessible cooking! Even my dad (known tofu hater) rubbernecked at it in the kitchen."

—Jack

SWEET POTATO HASH WITH TOFU

VEGAN

time 55 minutes

yield 2 to 3 servings

Hash, which comes from the French word for chop, can be made of any number of meats and proteins that cook and crisp on the stovetop. One of the most common might be corned beef and potato hash, but this recipe is more hands-off: It cooks on a sheet pan. This vegan hash is sweet, smoky and spicy, with cubes of sweet potato, tofu, peppers and onions. The potatoes and tofu are spunky with chili powder and crisp from cornstarch. Serve the dish for breakfast or dinner, with vinegary red onions for crunch, plus your favorite hash toppings.

—Ali Slagle

1 red bell pepper, cut into ½-inch pieces

1 red onion, three-quarters cut into ½-inch pieces, the rest thinly sliced

1 rosemary sprig (optional)

4 tablespoons extra-virgin olive oil

Kosher salt, such as Diamond Crystal

1 (14- to 16-ounce) block extra-firm tofu, cut into ½-inch pieces and patted very dry

8 ounces sweet potato, cut into ½-inch pieces

2 tablespoons cornstarch

2¼ teaspoons chili powder

1 tablespoon apple cider vinegar or lime juice

Fried or poached eggs, cilantro, parsley, hot sauce, shredded Cheddar, crumbled feta and/or ketchup, for serving (optional)

1. Place a rack in the lower third of the oven, heat the oven to 425 degrees and line a sheet pan with parchment. In a medium bowl, toss the bell pepper, ½-inch pieces of red onion and the rosemary (if using) with 2 tablespoons oil. Season with a pinch of salt, then arrange in a single layer on about one-quarter of the prepared sheet pan.
2. In the same bowl, combine the tofu, sweet potato, cornstarch and 2 teaspoons chili powder and season generously with about 2 teaspoons salt. Toss gently until well coated, then add the remaining 2 tablespoons oil and toss to coat. Arrange in a single layer next to the pepper and onion. Roast until the vegetables are tender and the tofu is crisp underneath, 30 to 35 minutes.
3. Meanwhile, in a small bowl, toss the sliced onion with the vinegar, remaining ¼ teaspoon chili powder and a pinch of salt. Serve the hash topped with the pickled onions and any additional toppings you like.

BREAKFAST UDON

time 40 minutes

yield 4 servings

This bowl of udon is inspired by the delicate noodle dishes often served as the first meal of the day in Japan. A light, savory broth of dashi, soy sauce and mirin provides a gentle kick start to your morning. Dashi, a simple seaweed-based stock, is foundational to many Japanese dishes, bolstering umami and lending balance. If you have 10 minutes and a piece of dried kombu in your pantry, make a quick kombu dashi (see Tip), but in a pinch, a lightly seasoned vegetable stock works, too. The jammy seven-minute egg and wilted spinach are enough to make this dish feel substantial, though you could also add slices of pan-fried tofu, tempura vegetable, seaweed or other hearty toppings to transform this into a complete weeknight dinner.

—Hetty Lui McKinnon

For the noodles

Salt

28 ounces precooked, vacuum-sealed udon, or 12 ounces dried udon

8 ounces fresh spinach

4 large eggs

2 scallions, thinly sliced

4 teaspoons sesame seeds

For the shoyu broth

2 tablespoons sesame oil

4 garlic cloves, grated

1 (2-inch) piece fresh ginger, peeled and grated

4 cups dashi (see Tip) or vegetable stock, store-bought or homemade (page 224)

¼ cup shoyu (Japanese soy sauce) or soy sauce

1 tablespoon mirin or sake

2 teaspoons fine sea salt

2 teaspoons granulated sugar

Tip

To make the kombu dashi, place ⅓ ounce dried kombu (about one 5 by 6-inch sheet) and 4¼ cups water in a pot and bring to a very low simmer over medium-low heat. Remove from heat and remove the kombu. (Reserve it for salads.) This will yield about 4 cups dashi.

1. Prepare the noodles: Bring a large pot of salted water to a boil. Add the noodles and cook according to package instructions until al dente. Place a colander in the sink and using a slotted spoon or tongs, transfer the noodles to the colander and run under cold water to stop the noodles from cooking further. Drain again.
2. Add the spinach to the same pot of water. Cook for about 1 minute, until the leaves are wilted but still bright green. Drain through a colander, emptying the water from pot, and run the spinach under cold water. Squeeze out as much liquid as possible, then scrunch the spinach into a ball and slice.
3. Fill the same pot with enough water to submerge the eggs. Bring to a boil over medium-high heat. Add the eggs, reduce heat to medium to keep the water at a gentle rolling simmer, and cook for 8 minutes. (This will give you a just-set yolk; for a runnier yolk, remove after 7 minutes.) Remove eggs from the water

"Quick, delicious, and the whole family loved it. I used marinated tofu instead of eggs to make it vegan. I can't believe it never occurred to me to have soup for breakfast!"

—Charis

immediately and run under cold water until the egg is cold to the touch. Place the eggs in a bowl of cold water.

4. Divide the udon noodles among four large bowls.
5. Prepare the broth: In a large pot, heat the sesame oil over medium heat, then add the garlic and ginger and cook for about 30 seconds, until fragrant. Add the remaining broth ingredients, along with 2 cups water. Bring to a boil. Once boiling, reduce heat and gently simmer for 4 to 5 minutes to allow the flavors to meld.
6. Peel the eggs and slice them in half lengthwise. Ladle the hot broth over the noodles. Top each bowl with a mound of spinach, 2 egg halves, scallions and sesame seeds.

"Amazing recipe. The ginger is like Lebowski's rug, tying the whole room/recipe together. My mornings have been changed for the better!"

—O.

GREEN SMOOTHIE

VEGAN

time 10 minutes

yield 1 (16-ounce) smoothie

For a green smoothie that's neither too sweet nor reminiscent of gazpacho, make the "Stew" from Veggies Natural Juice Bar & Cafe in Brooklyn. Fresh, spicy and sweet everyday staples like agave or honey, greens, ginger and banana harmonize thanks to one ingredient that brings them all together: vanilla extract, which enhances and balances flavors in baked goods and beyond. The Stew was invented on Veggies' opening day, when a customer named Stew asked for a drink using a few requested ingredients. The owners, Ian Callender and Jahman McKenzie, named the smoothie after him, also paying tribute to Caribbean stews. Mr. Callender advises not to add more liquid to this smoothie—the greens bring their own—or more vanilla or ginger, which can overpower. The proportions for this recipe have been fine-tuned over time.

—Ali Slagle

½ cup unsweetened nondairy milk (almond, oat, soy or hemp)

1 tablespoon agave or honey, plus more to taste

2 packed cups spinach leaves

1½ packed cups torn curly kale leaves (from about 2 leaves)

1 thin slice/3 grams peeled fresh ginger

1 large ripe banana

½ cup ice cubes

1 teaspoon pure vanilla extract

1. Place the milk, agave, spinach, kale, ginger, and banana in a blender and blend on high until smooth.
2. Add the ice and vanilla and blend on high again until smooth. Taste and add more agave, if desired.

GOAT CHEESE AND DILL DUTCH BABY

time 45 minutes

yield 6 servings

This savory Dutch baby—a dish that is typically sweet—is made by pouring a light, eggy batter into a heated pan of hot melted butter. The herb-flecked batter begins cooking on contact and, when baked, puffs and crisps and develops a tender, custard-like center. Adorned with crumbled goat cheese, fresh dill and crunchy watercress, the Dutch baby is finished with a drizzle of honey and a sprinkle of lemon juice. Served for breakfast or brunch, this one-pan meal is about as quick and straightforward as you can get.

—Yewande Komolafe

1 cup/148 grams crumbled plain goat cheese

½ cup chopped fresh dill, plus picked fronds for garnish

2 tablespoons olive oil

1 lemon

Coarse kosher salt and black pepper

1 cup/130 grams all-purpose flour

8 large eggs

¾ cup/190 milliliters whole milk

4 tablespoons/57 grams unsalted butter

2 cups watercress leaves with tender stems or other tender greens, such as spinach or arugula

1 tablespoon honey

1. In a small bowl, combine the goat cheese, ¼ cup dill and 1 tablespoon oil. Zest the lemon over the mixture, season with a pinch each of salt and pepper and let sit to marinate.
2. Place a rack in the lower third of the oven and heat oven to 425 degrees. In a large bowl, whisk together the flour, ½ teaspoon salt and ¼ teaspoon pepper. Add remaining ¼ cup dill and stir. In a separate large bowl, whisk together the eggs and milk. Whisk the wet ingredients into the dry until just combined.
3. In a large heavy oven-safe skillet, melt the butter over medium-high heat. Let it cook until it smells nutty and browns, about 5 minutes, swirling the skillet so that butter coats the bottom and sides of the pan.
4. Pour the batter into the hot buttered skillet and spoon half the marinated goat cheese into the center of the batter. Bake until puffed and golden, 20 to 22 minutes.
5. Cool the Dutch baby slightly in the pan, 5 to 6 minutes. To serve, top with watercress and dill fronds. Spoon remaining goat cheese on top and drizzle with honey and remaining 1 tablespoon oil. Slice the lemon and squeeze a wedge over the greens. Serve immediately.

"A triumph. Followed the recipe exactly and it puffed up magnificently—a bit of a showstopper."

—Kaziah

"I've been trying to eat more vegetables, so I thought adding Swiss chard to my breakfast would be a good move. WOW. This was so delicious, I texted two people about it immediately."

—Julia

GREEN SHAKSHUKA WITH AVOCADO AND LIME

time 35 minutes

yield 4 servings

This easy twist on classic North African shakshuka (traditionally eggs baked in tomato-pepper sauce, with cumin, paprika and cayenne) starts with a mixture of onion, garlic and chard sautéed until gently wilted: a nest of sorts for steam-poaching eggs. Once the eggs go in, be sure to keep the flame low and the pan covered so the eggs stay soft and almost oozy at their yolk. The chard and the half-and-half create a sort of light broth at the bottom of the shakshuka, which holds so much flavor and is one of the dish's charms. Lastly, be daring with smoked hot sauce at the end: It'll push the creamy avocado, cheese and eggs to their peak.

—Sarah Copeland

3 tablespoons olive oil

1 yellow onion, thinly sliced

2 garlic cloves, thinly sliced

1 large bunch/1½ pounds Swiss chard, stems and leaves separated and chopped

Kosher salt, such as Diamond Crystal

⅓ cup half-and-half or heavy cream

8 large eggs

Black pepper

3 ounces Cotija cheese or queso fresco, crumbled (about ¾ cup)

1 ripe Hass avocado, sliced

1 small jalapeño, thinly sliced

Chopped fresh cilantro

Smoked hot sauce, for serving

Corn tortillas, toasted, for serving

Lime wedges, for serving

1. In a large cast-iron skillet, heat the oil over medium-low heat. Add the onion and cook until softening, 5 minutes. Add the garlic and cook until fragrant, 5 minutes more.
2. Increase heat to medium-high, add the chard stems and cook to release some liquid, 5 minutes. Add the chard leaves, in batches, adding more as they wilt, and continue cooking, stirring occasionally, until completely wilted, 3 to 5 minutes more. Season with ½ teaspoon salt, pour in the half-and-half and stir loosely together.
3. With the back of a spoon, make eight small hollows in the cooked chard. Gently crack an egg into each hollow. Cover with a lid or foil (see Tip) and reduce heat to medium-low. Cook until the eggs are just set but still soft, 7 to 9 minutes. Remove the lid and sprinkle with salt and pepper. Scatter the Cotija, avocado, jalapeño and cilantro over top. Serve with smoked hot sauce, toasted tortillas and lime wedges.

Tip

Some cast-iron skillets come with a matching lid, which is useful for making the skillet operate a bit like a mini stovetop oven, cooking evenly and basting the food with flavor and steam. If you don't have one, use a lid from another pan, or two layers of thick foil large enough to cover your pan.

ZUCCHINI MUFFINS WITH CINNAMON CRUNCH TOPPING

time 45 minutes, plus cooling

yield 12 muffins

A touch of honey complements the nutty flavor of the whole wheat flour in these muffins. The zucchini and applesauce provide moisture and flavor, and the crunchy cinnamon topping makes for the perfect textural contrast against the soft cake. These muffins are a great addition to your morning cup of coffee. Store them on the counter, uncovered, to help preserve their crunchy coating. They also freeze well and can be reheated in a low-temperature oven or thawed at room temperature.

—Jerrelle Guy

2 tablespoons/28 grams unsalted butter, softened, plus ½ cup/114 grams unsalted butter, melted

2 medium zucchini (about 1 pound)

1 cup/120 grams plus 1 tablespoon whole wheat flour

1¼ cups/160 grams all-purpose flour

¾ cup/150 grams granulated sugar

2½ teaspoons baking powder

1 teaspoon kosher salt, such as Diamond Crystal

⅔ cup/160 milliliters whole milk, at room temperature

½ cup/120 milliliters unsweetened applesauce

¼ cup/60 milliliters honey

2 large eggs, at room temperature, beaten

1 tablespoon fresh lemon juice

2 teaspoons pure vanilla extract

⅓ cup/65 grams turbinado sugar

1 tablespoon ground cinnamon

1. Heat the oven to 400 degrees. Using 1 tablespoon/14 grams softened butter, generously butter the cups and the top of a standard 12-cup muffin tin. Set aside.
2. Cut the tips off the zucchini and grate the zucchini into shreds on a box grater. Pile the zucchini onto a clean dish towel and squeeze tightly over the sink to remove any excess water. Set aside.
3. In a large bowl, sift 1 cup of the whole wheat flour with the all-purpose flour, granulated sugar, baking powder and salt, then whisk to combine. Set aside.
4. In a medium bowl, whisk together the melted butter, milk, applesauce, honey, eggs, lemon juice and vanilla until combined. Make a well in the center of the dry ingredients and pour in the wet ingredients. Using a rubber spatula, gently fold everything together, being careful not to overmix. Fold everything until mostly combined, then sprinkle the zucchini over the top, breaking up any clumps with your hands, and finish folding the batter until combined. Using a spoon or scoop, divide the batter evenly among the muffin cups. (The batter should come to the top of each cup.)

"These were a big hit at my house. I had some pecans that I toasted and added."

—**Houston500**

5. In a small bowl, combine remaining 1 tablespoon whole wheat flour with the turbinado sugar and cinnamon. Using your fingers, work in remaining 1 tablespoon softened butter. Sprinkle the mixture over the tops, then brush away any crumbs that spill onto the muffin tin.
6. Bake the muffins, rotating halfway through, until the tops form firm domes, the sugar topping caramelizes and the muffins are cooked through, 24 to 26 minutes. (The tops should spring back when lightly pressed.) Remove from the oven and let cool in the tin for 15 minutes. Using a small offset spatula, transfer the muffins to a wire rack to cool for at least another 10 minutes. Serve warm or at room temperature.

"This was *really* good. I made double the sauce and used most of it. It's really the kind of dish that people who don't like tofu would like."

—**Corin**

TOFU SCRAMBLE

VEGAN

time 15 to 45 minutes

yield 4 servings

This quick egg-free scramble is a combination of flavors and textures that will surprise and delight tofu lovers and doubters alike. Soy sauce, turmeric and cumin provide bold seasoning, while searing the slabs of tofu on both sides before breaking it up yields plenty of crispy bits as well as tender ones. You can add cooked vegetables, leafy greens, beans, cheese or nutritional yeast with the scallions in Step 4, though you may want to increase the seasoning depending on the amount of extras you add. You can also swap in hot sauce, mustard or tahini for the soy sauce and play around with spice combinations, but don't skip the splash of water—it helps the tofu soak up all the flavors. Serve with toast, in place of eggs in a breakfast burrito or with a salad or breakfast potatoes.

—Ali Slagle

1 (14-ounce) block firm or extra-firm tofu

1 tablespoon low-sodium soy sauce or tamari

½ teaspoon ground turmeric

½ teaspoon ground cumin

Salt and black pepper

2 tablespoons canola oil

2 scallions, thinly sliced

1. Cut the block of tofu in half horizontally as you would a hamburger bun. Pat both pieces dry and wrap in paper towels or a clean dish towel. If time allows, press the tofu by placing a cast-iron skillet or other heavy object on top of the wrapped tofu for about 30 minutes. (This helps remove moisture so the tofu retains its shape better during cooking.)
2. In a measuring cup or small bowl, combine the soy sauce, turmeric and cumin with 2 tablespoons water.
3. Unwrap the tofu and season on all sides with salt and pepper. In a medium skillet, heat the oil, then cook the tofu over medium-high heat until golden brown and crisp on the bottom, 3 to 4 minutes. Flip the tofu and cook until golden brown and crisp on the other side, another 3 to 4 minutes. If the tofu is releasing water, hold the tofu with a spatula and pour off the water.
4. Reduce heat to medium. Using a spatula or wooden spoon, break up the tofu into chunks. Add the scallions and the soy sauce mixture and cook, stirring and continuing to break up the tofu, until absorbed, about 2 minutes. Serve immediately.

MORE-VEGETABLE-THAN-EGG FRITTATA

time 30 minutes

yield 2 or 4 servings

This simple frittata—just eggs, vegetables, fresh herbs and a little Parmesan if you're feeling luxurious—is proof that eating well doesn't have to be deprivational. It can also be delicious.

—Mark Bittman

2 tablespoons olive oil

½ onion, sliced (optional)

Salt and black pepper

4 to 6 cups any chopped or sliced raw or barely cooked vegetables, such as asparagus, spinach, zucchini, broccoli, potatoes, peas, peppers or onions

¼ cup fresh basil or parsley leaves, or 1 teaspoon chopped fresh tarragon or mint leaves, or any other herb

2 or 3 large eggs

½ cup freshly grated Parmesan cheese (optional)

1. In a large skillet (preferably nonstick or well-seasoned cast iron), heat the oil over medium heat. When hot, add the onion (if using) and cook, sprinkling with salt and pepper, until it is soft, 3 to 5 minutes. Add the vegetables, increase heat to medium-high and cook, stirring occasionally until they soften, from a couple of minutes for greens to 15 minutes for sliced potatoes. Adjust heat so vegetables brown a little without scorching. (With precooked vegetables, just add them to the onion and stir before proceeding.)
2. When the vegetables are nearly done, reduce heat to low and add the basil. Cook, stirring occasionally, until the vegetables are tender.
3. Meanwhile, in a small bowl beat the eggs with some salt and pepper, along with the Parmesan (if using). Pour over the vegetables, distributing the eggs evenly. Cook, undisturbed, until the eggs are barely set, 10 minutes or so; place the pan under the broiler for a minute or two if the top does not set. Cut frittata into wedges and serve hot, warm or at room temperature.

"This is a delicious and versatile recipe. I like to add halved grape tomatoes just before the eggs. They add a brightness to the flavor and make the frittata much prettier."

—Sue

MAKE-AHEAD EGG, SPINACH AND FETA WRAPS

time 55 minutes

yield 5 wraps

Packed with protein, enough baby spinach to make Popeye proud, and punchy umami from sun-dried tomatoes and feta cheese, these wraps are ideal for make-ahead breakfasts. Feel free to customize by adding herbs like dill, parsley or cilantro or a small handful of chopped roasted red peppers or pitted olives. The frittata-like egg mixture is baked in a baking pan and sliced into rectangles to fit easily on lavash wraps or burrito-size flour tortillas. If you don't want to make wraps, you can simply serve the tender frittata by itself.

—Naz Deravian

Cooking spray or neutral oil

¼ cup finely chopped sun-dried tomatoes, plus 3 tablespoons oil from the jar (see Tips)

1 yellow onion, finely chopped

Kosher salt, such as Diamond Crystal

5 to 6 ounces baby spinach (5 to 6 cups packed)

Black pepper

10 large eggs

3 ounces crumbled feta

5 lavash wraps (about 10 by 12 inches) or burrito-size flour tortillas, at room temperature (see Tips)

Cream cheese, fresh goat cheese or flavored soft cheese, such as Boursin (optional)

1. Spray a 9-by-13-inch baking pan with cooking spray, making sure to spray the sides well. Line the pan with parchment paper, leaving overhang on at least two sides, and spray the parchment paper with cooking spray. Place a rack in the center of the oven and heat the oven to 375 degrees.
2. In a large skillet, heat the sun-dried tomato oil over medium heat. Add the onion and cook, stirring frequently, until golden, 8 to 10 minutes. Sprinkle with a little salt, add the sundried tomatoes and cook for 2 minutes, stirring frequently. Add the spinach, in batches if necessary, and cook, stirring frequently, just until wilted. (You don't want the spinach to release any liquid.) Season with salt and pepper, keeping in mind you will also season the eggs. Remove from heat.
3. In a large bowl, season the eggs with 1 teaspoon salt and ¼ teaspoon pepper and beat with a whisk or fork until combined. Add the spinach mixture to the eggs and mix to combine. Wipe out the skillet and set aside. Transfer the egg mixture to the baking pan, spreading it out evenly. Top with the feta and bake until the eggs are fully set and the cheese is melted, 10 to 15 minutes. Remove from the oven and let rest for 2 minutes.
4. Slide the frittata onto a cutting board. Slice the frittata crosswise into 5 equal rectangles (each about 2½ inches wide). Place a lavash wrap on a work surface and spread with cream cheese (if using). Place a slice of frittata on the lavash,

Tips

Instead of sun-dried tomato oil, you can substitute olive oil.

Cold lavash is harder to wrap and can tear, so be sure to take the lavash out of the fridge a few minutes before wrapping.

leaving a 2-inch border at the bottom. Bring the sides of the lavash in and then fold up the bottom, rolling up the lavash like a flat burrito. Repeat with the remaining lavash and frittata.

5. Return the same skillet to medium heat. Spray each lavash wrap lightly with cooking spray on both sides. Place seam side down in the pan and cook until the lavash is warmed through and slightly golden on each side, 3 to 4 minutes per side. (Take care not to overcook it, or the lavash will become brittle.) Slice in half, on the diagonal if you like, and serve. (To make ahead, wrap the pan-cooked egg wraps in foil and refrigerate for up to 3 days or freeze for up to 3 months. Reheat in the microwave, in a skillet over low heat or in the oven at 350 degrees.)

"My kids deemed these the best pancakes that they have ever eaten. Light and fluffy, with a lovely flavor."

—Stephanie

LEMON RICOTTA PANCAKES

time 20 minutes

yield 8 to 10 small pancakes

This quick batter cooks into tender pancakes for the most comforting breakfast. Milky ricotta and butter, along with tangy buttermilk, lend a soft, sweet creaminess, and well-beaten eggs keep the pancakes fluffy and light. Lemon- and vanilla-scented sugar makes the pancakes sweet enough to eat on their own, but they're fun to serve with blueberry syrup or your favorite toppings. If you prefer soufflé-like pancakes, separate the egg whites from the yolks and beat them to stiff peaks. Mix the yolks in with the wet ingredients, fold the whipped whites in after the dry ingredients are incorporated and cook as directed below.

—Genevieve Ko

¾ cup/102 grams all-purpose flour

1½ teaspoons baking powder

¾ teaspoon fine sea salt

¼ cup/50 grams granulated sugar

1 lemon

1½ teaspoons pure vanilla extract

3 large eggs

¾ cup/170 grams whole milk ricotta

¼ cup/61 grams buttermilk, preferably whole milk

2 tablespoons/28 grams unsalted butter, melted, plus more at room temperature for cooking and serving

Blueberry syrup (see Tip), or other toppings, for serving (optional)

Tip

To make the syrup, combine 1 cup blueberries and 1 tablespoon lemon juice in a saucepan over medium heat for 2 minutes. Reduce the heat to medium-low, and reduce for 5 minutes more. Add ⅓ cup maple syrup, 1 cup blueberries and simmer for 5 minutes, stirring occasionally. Add more syrup if desired for consistency.

1. In a small bowl, whisk together the flour, baking powder and salt. Heat a griddle or a large nonstick or well-seasoned cast-iron skillet over medium-low heat.
2. Place the sugar in a large bowl, then finely grate the zest of the lemon directly over the sugar.
3. Using your fingers, gently rub the zest into the sugar.
4. Whisk in the vanilla to evenly moisten, then add the eggs and whisk until foamy on top.
5. Whisk in the ricotta, buttermilk and melted butter until well blended.
6. Add the flour mixture and gently stir until no traces of flour remain.
7. Generously butter the griddle, then drop a scant ¼ cup batter onto it. Repeat, spacing the rounds at least an inch apart. Cook until golden brown on the bottom and bubbling on top, 2 to 3 minutes.
8. Flip and cook until golden brown on the other side, about 2 minutes more. Repeat with more butter and the remaining batter. Serve warm, slathered with butter and drizzled with blueberry syrup or other toppings, if you'd like.

CHEESY POTATO BREAKFAST TACOS

time 35 minutes

yield 4 servings

Inspired by Mexican guisados, where proteins are sautéed in a sofrito of tomato and chiles, these cheesy breakfast tacos showcase Mexican home cooking at its best. Potatoes, poblanos and leeks are cooked simply with a grated tomato that caramelizes as it cooks down, giving an earthiness that combines with the smokiness of the poblano for an umami-packed medley. Mixed into scrambled eggs, topped with cheese and served family-style in a skillet alongside fresh corn or flour tortillas, this is a hearty, crowd-pleasing vegetarian breakfast (or breakfast for dinner!) that's endlessly satisfying.

—Kristina Felix

2 tablespoons unsalted butter

1 tablespoon neutral oil, such as grapeseed or avocado oil

2 medium or 1 large white potato (12 to 16 ounces), peeled and diced small

1 medium leek, white and light green parts only, thinly sliced, or 1 white onion, diced

1 poblano chile, diced small (seeded, if desired)

Kosher salt, such as Diamond Crystal, and black pepper

1 medium ripe tomato

4 large eggs

2 ounces mild semi-soft cheese, such as Chihuahua or Monterey Jack, grated

8 to 10 corn or flour tortillas, preferably fresh

Chopped scallions, cilantro or chives, for serving (optional)

Salsa negra or hot sauce, for serving (optional)

1. In a large cast-iron skillet or other heavy pan, heat 1 tablespoon butter and the oil over medium-high heat. When the butter melts, add the potatoes, leek, poblano, 1 teaspoon salt and ½ teaspoon pepper and cook, stirring occasionally, until the potatoes start to soften, about 9 minutes.
2. While the potatoes are cooking, cut the tomato in half and, using a box grater set in a bowl, grate the cut sides of the tomato down to the peel. Discard peels. This should result in ¾ to 1 cup grated tomato. Reduce heat to medium, add the grated tomato and ½ teaspoon salt to the vegetables in the pan and mix to combine. Cook until the liquid evaporates and the tomato begins to caramelize, about 3 minutes.
3. Make a well in the middle of the pan and add remaining 1 tablespoon butter. In a medium bowl, whisk the eggs with ½ teaspoon salt. When the butter melts, add the eggs to the well and cook, mixing occasionally, until almost set, about 7 minutes. Combine the eggs with the potato mixture in the pan, turn off the heat and sprinkle the cheese on top.
4. Meanwhile, heat the tortillas (see Tip) and keep warm by placing them in a tortilla warmer or wrapping them in a clean dish towel.

Tip

To heat tortillas quickly, heat a comal, skillet or griddle over medium-high heat. Place as many stacks of 2 tortillas on your hot surface as will fit without overlapping too much and heat for 30 seconds. Carefully flip all the stacks, then flip the top tortilla of each stack so that the side that has not touched the hot surface faces up. Heat for another 30 seconds, then flip all the stacks again. Repeat the process until the tortillas are soft and warmed through and have touched the hot surface on both sides. For store-bought corn tortillas that feel a little dry, try lightly spraying them with water while they reheat.

"Love this recipe! If you're looking for the potatoes to cook quicker and to be more crunchy, I recommend boiling them first before cooking them off in the skillet!"

—Molly

5. Bring the skillet to the table along with the tortillas, scallions (if using) and salsa (if using) and let everyone assemble their own breakfast taco.

"This is now our preferred breakfast after tiring of oatmeal . . . The dal is very friendly toward leftover veggies—roasted cauliflower, Sichuan broccoli, braised eggplant."

—Mark L.

EVERYDAY DAL

time 15 minutes

yield 4 servings

The warming, soothing and downright healing effects of dal are well known throughout South Asia and its diaspora. This is an any time, any day dish for a good reason: It's simple to make but tastes complex, and the flavor only deepens over time. There are countless ways to make dal; this version requires just 10 minutes and 5 ingredients (not including salt), all serving important purposes: The lentils cook quickly, the turmeric lends an earthy wholesomeness and the rich chhonk, or tempering, made by sizzling spices with ghee, brings instant depth. To gussy it up, try adding a packet of frozen spinach or stirring minced garlic into the chhonk. If you're tempted to use ground cumin instead of cumin seeds, resist! The seeds have a distinctly smokier flavor and add a pleasant texture to the dal.

—Priya Krishna

1 cup red lentils (also known as red split lentils or masoor dal)

1 teaspoon ground turmeric

Kosher salt, such as Diamond Crystal

3 tablespoons ghee

2 teaspoons cumin seeds

⅛ to ¼ teaspoon ground red chile

⅛ teaspoon asafetida (optional but extremely good; see Tip)

Rice or roti, for serving

1. In a medium saucepan with a lid, combine the lentils (no need to rinse them) with the turmeric, 1 teaspoon salt and 3 cups water. If you like your dal a little soupier, add an extra cup of water. Bring to a boil over high heat, then reduce to a simmer, cover and cook for 5 to 8 minutes, until the lentils resemble a loose porridge. If the lentils are too thick, add a little hot water.
2. In a small pan or pot, melt the ghee over medium heat, then add the cumin seeds. Let them cook until they are aromatic and a darker shade of brown, about 1 minute. Stir in the chile powder and asafetida (if using), let them toast for a few seconds until fragrant (the asafetida will give off a garlic-esque scent), then remove from heat.
3. Taste the lentils and add more salt, if desired. Pour the hot ghee over the lentils—you can either stir to combine or leave it be for a dramatic presentation—and serve with rice or roti.

Tip

Asafetida is a tree resin commonly used as a seasoning in South Asian cuisines. It has a wonderfully potent, allium-esque flavor that adds depth to many dishes. It can be ordered online or found in South Asian grocery stores and is worth going out of your way for—it really makes this dish sing. An imperfect but somewhat suitable substitute is garlic powder.

CHAPTER 2

SALAD DAYS

It is impossible for me to hear "salad" and not think of *SpongeBob SquarePants.* In one episode, Mr. Krabs hires his daughter for a summer gig at his burger joint. She remakes the restaurant in her image: young, hip, pink. SpongeBob, meanwhile, is bewildered by her menu changes: "What in the name of Davy Jones's locker is a sah-lad?" he asks.

His question was astute, not naive. What is a salad, really?

Salads are boundless in their opportunities for interpretation. They aren't inherently righteous; you should never "have" to eat a salad. They should be exercises in joy! In abundance! My only rule for salads is that the assorted ingredients—vegetables, sure, but also fruits or beans or noodles or tofu—are united by dressing.

Consider the caprese. The pedants might say it is a fruit salad at best; the killjoys might say it's an effective Trojan horse for a couple dozen mozzarella soldiers. But it's still a salad.

That might explain my affinity for Hana Asbrink's Cold Tofu Salad with Tomatoes and Peaches (page 46), one of my favorite recipes in this whole book. Hana's salad looks suspiciously like a caprese but tastes like anything but. Lumps of jiggly, cooling silken tofu rest atop the fruit, adding heft and protein. A puckery dressing of balsamic and rice vinegars, soy sauce and sesame oil checks my single salad rule box, and a scattering of fresh basil and mint perfumes the dish.

In the pages ahead, you'll see staples like Dijon mustard, miso paste, nutritional yeast and caper brine transformed into revelatory dressings, as in Becky Hughes's Vegan Caesar Salad with Crisp Chickpeas (page 57). And you'll find that, for a stellar salad, lettuce is hardly a requirement. You won't miss it in inspired dishes like Yewande Komolafe's Roasted Vegetables with Creamy Coconut Dressing (page 70).

The recipes in this chapter steer into salad stereotypes head-on and make the case for calling just about anything coming out of your kitchen by that name. A bowl of vegetable dumplings? A verdantly topped pizza? That's sah-lad, baby.

DUMPLING TOMATO SALAD WITH CHILE CRISP VINAIGRETTE
PAGE 48

EXTRA-GREEN PASTA SALAD
PAGE 51

NO-COOK CHILI BEAN SALAD
PAGE 52

BROWN BUTTER LENTIL AND SWEET POTATO SALAD
PAGE 54

VEGAN CAESAR SALAD WITH CRISP CHICKPEAS
PAGE 57

SALAD PIZZA WITH WHITE BEANS AND PARMESAN
PAGE 58

COLD TOFU SALAD WITH TOMATOES AND PEACHES
PAGE 61

MISO EGGPLANT SALAD WITH CHICKPEAS
PAGE 62

CORN AND MISO PASTA SALAD
PAGE 65

CHOPPED SALAD WITH JALAPEÑO-RANCH DRESSING
PAGE 66

QUINOA AND BROCCOLI SPOON SALAD
PAGE 69

ROASTED VEGETABLES WITH CREAMY COCONUT DRESSING
PAGE 70

SPICY CUCUMBERS WITH YOGURT, LEMON AND HERBS
PAGE 73

ORZO SALAD WITH LENTILS AND ZUCCHINI
PAGE 74

DUMPLING TOMATO SALAD WITH CHILE CRISP VINAIGRETTE

time 20 minutes

yield 4 servings

Harness the crowd-pleasing power of dumplings in this hearty yet light main course salad. The base is simple and summery: Ripe tomatoes are lightly touched with salt, garlic and basil, providing a perfectly fragrant canvas for pan-fried potsticker dumplings. Salting intensifies the tanginess and fruitiness of the tomatoes while coaxing out some of the juice, which becomes a light sauce for the dumplings. (Salting also works wonders for out-of-season tomatoes, meaning you could eat this salad all year round.) Use your favorite chile crisp, as it is the dominant flavor in the dressing and will greatly impact the final dish; crisp brands vary in saltiness and heat, so taste and season accordingly.

—Hetty Lui McKinnon

For the salad

2½ pounds ripe tomatoes (any variety), cut into 1- to 2-inch pieces, at room temperature

1 garlic clove, grated

½ cup fresh basil leaves, torn

Kosher salt, such as Diamond Crystal, and black pepper

Neutral oil, such as canola or vegetable oil

1 pound frozen vegetarian potsticker dumplings

1 to 2 tablespoons store-bought crispy fried shallots (optional)

For the chile crisp vinaigrette

3 tablespoons chile crisp (or chile oil)

2 tablespoons unseasoned rice vinegar

1 tablespoon soy sauce, or more to taste

1. Place the tomatoes on a large serving plate or in a bowl. Add the garlic, half the basil leaves, 1 teaspoon of salt and a big pinch of black pepper. Toss to combine, then set aside.
2. To make the vinaigrette, in a small bowl, combine the chile crisp, rice vinegar and soy sauce and whisk to combine. Taste and if it needs more saltiness, add ½ teaspoon more soy sauce.
3. Heat a large nonstick or well-seasoned cast-iron skillet with a lid over medium-high heat for 1 to 2 minutes until very hot. Add 1 to 2 tablespoons oil and, working in batches, add the dumplings, flat side down, and cook until the bottoms of the dumplings are lightly browned, 1 to 2 minutes. Immediately add about ¼ cup water to the pan, just enough to cover the base of the dumplings, then cover and cook until the water has evaporated, 3 to 4 minutes. Transfer the cooked dumplings to a plate and continue cooking remaining dumplings. (If you prefer to steam the dumplings, see Tip.)

Tip

To steam, arrange the dumplings in a steamer basket lined with parchment paper or cabbage leaves, place over a pan of boiling water and steam for 10 to 15 minutes.

> "As someone who struggles to eat traditional salads, I highly recommend this one. Super easy and tasty."
>
> **—Emma**

4. To serve, place the warm dumplings over the tomato salad and drizzle with the chile crisp vinaigrette. Toss very gently. Top with the crispy fried shallots (if using) and remaining ¼ cup basil leaves. Serve while the dumplings are either still warm or at room temperature.

"Loved the amount of produce packed into this recipe—perfect for spring & summer, and so delicious!"

—Shira K.

EXTRA-GREEN PASTA SALAD

time 30 minutes

yield 4 to 6 servings

This vibrant green pasta salad gets its color from a combination of spinach and basil, though you can swap the spinach for arugula to get a more peppery finish. (Some of us need a little bite in our lives!) The miso does a lot of the heavy lifting in the sauce, imparting a salty, almost Parmesan-like quality. You can eat the salad immediately or chilled for a summer picnic. If making it a day ahead, don't add the basil garnish and cheese until you're ready to serve.

—Andy Baraghani

Salt

1 pound short pasta, such as rigatoni, campanelle or fusilli

8 ounces sugar snap peas

1 cup frozen peas

3½ ounces baby spinach (about 3 packed cups)

1½ ounces basil leaves (about 2 packed cups), plus more for serving

½ cup extra-virgin olive oil

2 tablespoons white miso paste

1 garlic clove, crushed

1 lemon, zested and juiced

Black pepper

4 ounces Parmesan or other firm salty cheese, such as feta or aged Gouda, thinly sliced

1. Bring a large pot of water to a boil, then throw in a handful of salt. Add the pasta, give it a stir and cook until al dente. Just before draining, add the sugar snap peas and frozen peas to the boiling water to barely soften, 20 to 30 seconds. Drain the pasta and peas and rinse lightly with cold water. Set aside.
2. While the pasta water comes to a boil, place the spinach, basil, oil, miso, garlic and lemon zest and juice in a blender. Blend to a bright green purée. Taste and adjust seasoning with salt and a few grinds of pepper, then blend again.
3. Transfer the purée to a large bowl that is big enough to toss all the pasta. Add the pasta and peas and toss until coated. Season to taste with salt and pepper. Add the Parmesan and more basil leaves. Toss once more before serving.

NO-COOK CHILI BEAN SALAD

VEGAN

time 25 minutes

yield 4 servings

All the usual suspects found in a vegetarian bean chili appear in this salad—canned beans, tomato, bell pepper, red onion and spices—but there's no cooking-with-heat required. The tomatoes are salted to tenderize and coax out their sweet, umami juices. Cumin, coriander, smoked paprika and dried oregano inject smoky earthiness and complexity. While black and pinto beans are used here, it is absolutely viable to use whatever beans you have on hand for this pantry-friendly recipe. Best of all, the salad can be dressed up with the usual chili toppings, such as avocado, sour cream and cheese. Eat as is or with tortillas or corn chips on the side.

—Hetty Lui McKinnon

1 pound tomatoes, roughly chopped into 1-inch chunks

½ small red onion, finely diced

1 garlic clove, finely chopped

1 tablespoon red or white wine vinegar

Salt and black pepper

1 (15-ounce) can pinto beans, rinsed and drained

1 (15-ounce) can black beans, rinsed and drained

1 bell pepper, roughly chopped

1 teaspoon ground cumin

1 teaspoon ground coriander

1 teaspoon smoked paprika

1 teaspoon dried oregano

½ to 1 jalapeño, chopped

Handful of chopped fresh cilantro leaves

¼ cup extra-virgin olive oil, plus more as needed

1 lime, quartered

Any combination of corn chips, tortillas, sour cream, avocado and cheese (such as Cheddar, crumbled feta or queso blanco), for serving

1. Place the tomatoes, red onion, garlic, vinegar and 1 teaspoon salt in a large bowl and toss to combine. Leave to marinate for 5 to 10 minutes. Using your hands, squeeze the tomatoes to crush them roughly, extracting juice and softening them.
2. To the tomato mixture, add both types of beans, the bell pepper, cumin, coriander, smoked paprika, oregano, jalapeño, cilantro and ¼ cup olive oil; toss to combine. Taste and season with salt and pepper and more olive oil, if you like.
3. Divide the salad among four bowls. Serve with lime wedges on the side, and top with desired toppings.

"This is so awesome, and my new best friend for summer."

—**Claire B.**

BROWN BUTTER LENTIL AND SWEET POTATO SALAD

time 35 minutes

yield 4 to 6 servings

This simple lentil salad has a little secret: a toasty brown butter vinaigrette perfumed with sage. The dish has as much texture as it does flavor. French green lentils or black lentils are the ideal choice, as they hold their shape well after cooking, but brown lentils will work too, though they'll be a bit softer. Start testing your lentils for doneness after about 15 minutes; you want them cooked through but not mushy, and they're best if they retain some bite. Roasted until tender, the sweet potatoes add richness, but feel free to substitute just about any roasted vegetable. Carrots, beets or red bell peppers would all be delicious in their stead.

—Yossy Arefi

For the salad

1 pound sweet potatoes, butternut squash or carrots, peeled and cut into ¾-inch pieces (about 4 cups)

2 tablespoons olive oil

Salt and black pepper

1 cup French green or black lentils, rinsed

½ cup chopped fresh parsley leaves and tender stems

½ cup crumbled goat cheese (optional)

For the brown butter vinaigrette

1 tablespoon minced fresh sage leaves

4 tablespoons unsalted butter

1 tablespoon extra-virgin olive oil

2 tablespoons red wine vinegar

1 teaspoon pure maple syrup

Salt and black pepper

1. Place a rack in the center of the oven and heat the oven to 375 degrees.
2. Prepare the salad: On a baking sheet, toss the sweet potatoes with the oil and a sprinkle of salt and pepper. Spread into an even layer and roast, stirring occasionally, until golden and tender, 15 to 25 minutes.
3. While the sweet potatoes roast, cook the lentils. In a medium pot with a lid, cover the lentils with about 6 cups water. Salt the water generously and bring the mixture to a boil. Reduce heat to a simmer and cook the lentils until just tender, 15 to 25 minutes. Drain the lentils, then return them to the pot. Cover to keep warm.
4. Prepare the vinaigrette: Place the sage in a small bowl. In a small skillet, melt the butter over medium heat. (Use a pan with a light interior so you can easily see the milk solids change color.) Cook the butter for a few minutes, stirring occasionally and scraping the milk solids off the bottom and sides of the pan as needed, until the milk solids turn golden brown and smell toasty.

"This has become one of my favorite packable lunch options—I've made it with butternut squash, sweet potato and carrots, all to great result."

—EHC

5. Pour the hot browned butter and all the toasty bits over the sage; it will crackle and foam a bit. Let the mixture sit for 1 minute to let the foam subside, then whisk in the olive oil, vinegar and maple syrup. Season with salt and pepper to taste.
6. Add the cooked sweet potatoes to the pot with the warm lentils. Pour the dressing over the top and stir gently to combine. Add the parsley, season with more salt and pepper, if desired, and toss to combine.
7. Transfer the mixture to a serving dish and sprinkle with goat cheese (if using). Serve warm.

"Forget best vegan Caesar dressing—this is the best Caesar dressing I've tasted. Ever."

—Sarah G.

VEGAN CAESAR SALAD WITH CRISP CHICKPEAS

VEGAN

time 25 minutes

yield 2 to 4 servings

There are many ways to mimic the rich, creamy texture of emulsified egg-based Caesar dressing: tofu, vegan mayonnaise, aquafaba whipped with oil, the list goes on. Blended raw cashews prove themselves the best base in this version, which is fortified with garlic, mustard, miso paste and caper brine to achieve the tangy-salty-punchy balance found in the real deal. Crisp chickpeas and hand-torn croutons add a crunchiness that plays well with the velvety dressing.

—Becky Hughes

For the salad

½ small loaf crusty bread, such as sourdough, torn into 1-inch pieces (about 2 cups)

¼ cup extra-virgin olive oil

Kosher salt, such as Diamond Crystal, and black pepper

1 (15-ounce) can chickpeas, drained, rinsed and thoroughly dried

1 large bunch Tuscan kale, stems removed and leaves roughly chopped into 1-inch pieces (about 4 cups)

1 large head romaine lettuce, roughly chopped into 1-inch pieces (about 6 cups)

For the dressing

1 cup whole (unroasted) cashews

1 snack-size (2 by 3-inch) sheet roasted nori, crumbled (optional)

¼ cup nutritional yeast, plus more for serving

¼ cup fresh lemon juice (from 2 lemons)

3 garlic cloves

2 teaspoons brine from a jar of capers

1 teaspoon Dijon mustard

1 teaspoon white miso paste

¾ teaspoon kosher salt

½ teaspoon black pepper

1. Heat the oven to 400 degrees. On a sheet pan, toss the bread with 2 tablespoons oil. Season generously with salt and pepper. On a second baking sheet, toss the chickpeas with remaining 2 tablespoons oil and season generously with salt and pepper. Bake both until the chickpeas and croutons are browned and crisp, stirring halfway through, about 10 minutes for the croutons and 20 minutes for the chickpeas. Set aside.
2. While the chickpeas and croutons roast, prepare the dressing: In a high-speed blender, combine all the dressing ingredients, add ¾ cup water and blend until completely smooth, 3 to 4 minutes, scraping down the sides with a rubber spatula every now and again. Set dressing aside. You should have 1½ cups.
3. In a large bowl, combine the kale and the dressing. Using your hands, massage the kale until slightly softened. Add the lettuce, croutons and half the roasted chickpeas; toss to coat and season to taste with salt and pepper. Sprinkle with nutritional yeast and remaining roasted chickpeas. Grind black pepper over the top and serve immediately.

SALAD PIZZA WITH WHITE BEANS AND PARMESAN

time 45 minutes

yield 4 servings

Inspired by California Pizza Kitchen's tricolore salad pizza, this pizza features a mountain of brightly dressed greens and beans atop a crisp Parmesan crust. Rolling the dough very thin takes some patience, but the reward is a snappy crust similar to that of pizza tonda, a thin-crust pie that's popular in Rome. The salad is made of arugula, white beans and pickled pepperoncini, dressed simply with olive oil and the brine from the peppers, but any salad topping would do. (The C.P.K. original had radicchio, greens, tomatoes and a vinaigrette.) With an abundance of leaves atop, fold the slices in half to eat, or embrace the mess—it's all part of the fun.

—Ali Slagle

1 (15-ounce) can white beans, such as cannellini or Great Northern, rinsed

¼ cup sliced pickled pepperoncini (6 to 8 peppers), plus 2 tablespoons brine

2 tablespoons extra-virgin olive oil, plus more for greasing

Salt and black pepper

1 pound store-bought or homemade pizza dough, at room temperature, divided into two 8-ounce portions

1 cup freshly grated Parmesan, plus more for serving

3 to 5 ounces baby arugula

1. Place a sheet pan in the oven and heat the oven to 500 degrees.
2. In a large bowl, stir together the beans, pepperoncini, pickle brine and oil. Season with salt and pepper, then set aside.
3. Place a kitchen towel on a work surface, then place a second sheet pan upside down on the towel (or use a cutting board). (This will serve as your pizza peel; the towel stabilizes the setup as you roll the dough.) Lightly grease a piece of parchment with oil and place it, greased side down, on top of the upside-down sheet pan. With a lightly greased rolling pin, roll one-half of the dough on the parchment as thin as you can, about ⅛- to ¼-inch thick. (If the dough retracts, let it rest a few minutes before continuing.)
4. Sprinkle ½ cup Parmesan over the dough. Remove the preheated sheet pan from the oven and carefully slide the parchment with the dough onto the hot baking sheet. Cook until golden brown on the top and bottom, 10 to 12 minutes. Meanwhile, roll out the remaining dough on a second piece of greased parchment and cover with remaining ½ cup Parmesan. Transfer the first pizza to a cooling rack to crisp, then repeat with the second piece of dough.
5. Add the arugula to the bean mixture, season with salt and pepper, and toss gently to combine. Top each pizza with the salad, plus more grated or shaved Parmesan.

"This is fantastic with a drizzle of Mike's Hot Honey. Also added lemon zest and red pepper flakes. Will be making again and again."

—carley

"Terrific at the end of a 95-degree day like today! Mainly stayed with the recipe but this is really one of those non-recipe recipes, adaptable to your tastes."

—Outlier 101

COLD TOFU SALAD WITH TOMATOES AND PEACHES

VEGAN

time 20 minutes

yield 4 to 6 servings

Sweet, savory and refreshing for summer's hottest days, this is the salad to make when tomatoes and peaches are at their prime, on the verge of bursting. Inspired by Italian caprese salad and Japanese hiyayakko, it features juicy, ripe peach and tomato wedges seasoned with flaky salt, which draws out their juices to mingle with soy-balsamic dressing and creamy silken tofu. Top the salad with a shower of fragrant basil and mint, a nod to the shiso that often accompanies hiyayakko, and a few cranks of black pepper. Be sure to spoon the umami-rich dressing (the best part!) over the tomatoes, peaches and tofu so that it pools at the bottom of the serving platter.

—Hana Asbrink

For the salad

1 (12- to 14-ounce) block silken tofu, chilled

2 to 3 ripe medium peaches

3 to 4 ripe medium tomatoes

Flaky sea salt

¼ cup packed fresh basil leaves

2 tablespoons fresh mint leaves

Black pepper

For the dressing

3 tablespoons extra-virgin olive oil

1 tablespoon balsamic vinegar

1 tablespoon unseasoned rice vinegar

1 tablespoon toasted sesame oil

2 teaspoons soy sauce

1 teaspoon granulated sugar

1. Prepare the salad: Carefully drain the tofu in its packaging, then remove the tofu. Gently wrap it with paper towels or a clean kitchen towel to absorb excess moisture and set it on a plate.
2. Meanwhile, cut the peaches and tomatoes into 1-inch-thick wedges and place on a serving platter, pouring any tomato or peach juices from the cutting board over the dish. Season generously with salt to draw out juices.
3. Unwrap the tofu and return it to the plate. Using a large spoon, scoop mounds of tofu onto the tomatoes and peaches. Season the tofu with salt.
4. Prepare the dressing: In a small glass jar with a lid, combine dressing ingredients, cover and shake to combine. Spoon 4 tablespoons of the dressing over the salad. Extra dressing can be served alongside.
5. Just before serving, stack the basil and mint leaves and roughly chop. Top the salad with the chopped herbs and black pepper. Serve immediately, taking care to spoon extra dressing and juices from the bottom of the platter over the top.

MISO EGGPLANT SALAD WITH CHICKPEAS

VEGAN

time 35 minutes

yield 4 servings

The flawless flavor pairing found in the popular Japanese dish miso-glazed eggplant serves as inspiration for this bold and textural salad. For high-temperature roasting, cutting the eggplant into chunky pieces optimizes golden, crisp edges and a silky, buttery interior. The vinaigrette is a standout—punchy from the ginger, intensely savory from the miso, and with a sweet hum from the mirin. The simplicity of a salad founded on just eggplant and chickpeas makes this an excellent weeknight option, and there are many ways to add more heft: Incorporate a few handfuls of spinach, add some pan-fried or baked tofu (page 229) or toss with some cold soba noodles.

—Hetty Lui McKinnon

For the eggplant salad

2 tablespoons vegetable oil

1 tablespoon toasted sesame oil

2 pounds eggplant (about 3 small or 2 medium), trimmed and cut into 1-inch chunks

Salt and black pepper

2 (15-ounce) cans chickpeas, rinsed and drained

2 scallions, sliced

Toasted white sesame seeds, for serving

Cooked soba noodles, for serving

For the miso dressing

2 tablespoons white miso paste

2 tablespoons mirin

2 tablespoons toasted sesame oil

1 tablespoon rice vinegar

1 garlic clove, finely grated

1 (1-inch) piece fresh ginger, peeled and grated

1 teaspoon sugar

1. Heat the oven to 425 degrees.
2. Prepare the eggplant salad: In a small bowl, mix together the vegetable oil and sesame oil. Place the eggplant on a rimmed sheet pan and drizzle with the oil mixture. Season with salt and pepper and toss well to coat. Roast until the eggplant is tender, with golden edges, 20 to 25 minutes.
3. Meanwhile, make the dressing: Place the miso, mirin, sesame oil, vinegar, garlic, ginger and sugar in a large bowl and whisk to combine.
4. Add the eggplant to the dressing along with the chickpeas and scallions; toss to combine. Taste and season with salt and pepper. Top with sesame seeds and serve with soba noodles.

"Simple and nice. Great to use up garden eggplants!"

—Amanda N.

"This was unexpectedly delicious! I used preserved lemon because it's what I had on hand but all that actually matters is that I cannot stop eating this."

—**Jeremy**

CORN AND MISO PASTA SALAD

VEGAN

time 50 minutes

yield 4 to 6 servings

The interplay between the crunch of the celery, the chew of the pasta and the pop of the corn kernels makes this (potentially vegan) pasta salad a textural pleasure. Pasta salads that you can easily eat with a spoon reign supreme, and ditalini's petite shape—which mimics the size of fresh corn kernels—makes it the perfect pasta candidate. Miso adds savory notes and deep umami flavor to the mayonnaise dressing. This recipe calls for Calabrian chile, but the miso-mayo mix is versatile: You can substitute anything from chopped chipotles in adobo to a spoonful of gochujang for a hit of heat.

—Ham El-Waylly

Salt

8 ounces ditalini pasta

4 ears fresh corn, shucked

2 large celery stalks, finely chopped

⅔ cup finely minced fresh chives

Granulated sugar

4½ tablespoons white or yellow miso paste

4½ tablespoons fresh lemon juice (from about 2 lemons), plus more to taste

1½ tablespoons finely chopped Calabrian chiles, minced chipotles in adobo, gochujang or sambal oelek, plus more to taste

½ cup vegan (or regular) mayonnaise

1. Bring a medium pot of salted water to a boil over high heat. Add the pasta and cook according to package instructions until al dente. Drain the pasta and rinse under cold water until cool. Drain again and set aside.
2. Grab a large bowl and invert a smaller bowl inside of it. Hold the corn upright on the center of the smaller bowl. Using a sharp chef's knife, slice downward to shave the kernels off the cob. Discard the cobs and remove the smaller bowl. Place the pasta, celery and chives in the large bowl. Season with a large pinch of salt and a pinch of sugar and toss to combine.
3. In the smaller bowl, whisk the miso, lemon juice and chiles to combine. Add the mayonnaise and whisk until fully incorporated.
4. Combine the dressing with the corn mixture and toss. Taste and adjust seasoning with more lemon juice, chiles, salt or sugar as needed. Store, refrigerated in an airtight container, for up to 3 days.

CHOPPED SALAD WITH JALAPEÑO-RANCH DRESSING

time 20 minutes

yield 4 to 6 servings

This chopped salad is fresh, festive and excessive in a celebratory way. While most salads opt for the lightest layer of dressing to optimize flavors of the produce, this one calls for the dressing to generously coat the crisp ingredients. The final result is punchy and satisfying, combining rich ingredients, like avocado, Cotija and a mayonnaise-thickened dressing with those with bite, like radishes, corn kernels and tortilla chips. This salad eschews subtlety and hits all the right notes.

—Alexa Weibel

For the dressing

½ cup buttermilk

½ cup mayonnaise

3 large scallions, finely chopped

⅓ cup finely chopped fresh cilantro

2 tablespoons finely chopped jalapeño (seeded, if desired)

Zest of 1 lime

½ teaspoon onion powder

¼ teaspoon garlic powder

Kosher salt, such as Diamond Crystal, and black pepper

For the salad

3 romaine lettuce hearts (about 1 pound), chopped into bite-size pieces

3 ears fresh corn, shucked, kernels removed from cobs

8 radishes, halved lengthwise and thinly sliced into half-moons

2 large ripe Hass avocados, diced

5 scallions, thinly sliced at an angle

½ cup crumbled Cotija cheese or grated Parmesan

1 cup chopped fresh cilantro leaves and tender stems

Kosher salt and black pepper

2 cups crumbled lime-flavored tortilla chips (optional)

1. Prepare the dressing: In a large measuring cup, whisk together the buttermilk, mayonnaise, scallions, cilantro, jalapeño, lime zest, onion powder and garlic powder. Season with ¾ teaspoon salt and ½ teaspoon black pepper. (You should have 1¼ cups. The dressing will taste quite salty at this point and that is intentional. You want it to hold up when tossed with a big pile of vegetables.)
2. Prepare the salad: In a large shallow bowl or on a platter, toss the romaine with half of the following ingredients: corn, radishes, avocados, sliced scallions, Cotija and cilantro. Taste and season with salt and pepper. Add ½ cup dressing and toss to coat. Season again with salt and pepper.

"Made this last night, and the family raved! Quote from my MIL: 'Do not lose this recipe.'"

—Donna

3. Top with remaining corn, radishes, avocados, scallions, Cotija and cilantro, scattering the garnishes on top or arranging them in stripes or piles. Sprinkle some crumbled tortilla chips on top, if using. Drizzle the salad with an additional ¼ cup dressing and serve immediately, with any remaining dressing and additional tortilla chips alongside.

"Really delicious, and certain to become a weekday lunch favorite. I was pleasantly surprised with how quickly the broccoli 'cured' in the dressing."

—Gigi

QUINOA AND BROCCOLI SPOON SALAD

time 30 minutes

yield 4 to 6 servings

This easy chopped salad fits loads of texture and flavor onto a spoon by combining finely chopped raw broccoli with chewy dried cranberries, crunchy pecans, fluffy quinoa and chunks of sharp Cheddar cheese. The mixture is tossed in a punchy mustard vinaigrette that soaks into the florets, only getting better as it sits. Feel free to substitute the quinoa for any grain, like brown rice, farro or buckwheat groats, though the cook time may vary.

—Sohla El-Waylly

Salt

1 cup quinoa, rinsed

1 lemon

3 tablespoons extra-virgin olive oil

3 tablespoons Dijon mustard

2 tablespoons honey

2 tablespoons apple cider vinegar

Black pepper

1 large head broccoli (about 1½ pounds)

1 medium tart, crisp apple

4 ounces sharp Cheddar

¾ cup toasted pecans, roughly chopped

½ cup dried cranberries

1. Bring a medium pot of water to a boil over high heat and season aggressively with salt. Add the quinoa, then reduce heat to maintain a simmer. Cook until plump and tender, about 15 minutes. Transfer to a fine-mesh sieve, rinse with cool water and drain well.
2. While the quinoa cooks, finely grate the zest of the lemon into a large bowl, then cut the lemon in half. Add the oil, mustard, honey and vinegar, plus the juice of ½ lemon and whisk together. Season with salt and pepper to taste.
3. Peel the stem of the broccoli and trim the dry end. Finely chop the entire head of broccoli and add to the dressing. Finely chop the apple and the cheese, then add to the bowl and toss to combine.
4. Add the cooked quinoa, nuts and cranberries and toss to combine. Taste and add more salt, pepper and lemon juice, as needed. Store, refrigerated, for up to 3 days.

ROASTED VEGETABLES WITH CREAMY COCONUT DRESSING

VEGAN

time 1 hour 5 minutes

yield 4 servings

A creamy, tangy dressing enlivens this warm salad of roasted carrots, beets and fennel. Coconut cream adds a lovely richness to the vinaigrette while ginger brings bite and rice vinegar and lime deliver a slight pucker. To achieve golden-brown caramelization, make sure the cut vegetables are dry and spread evenly on the sheet pan. And those fennel fronds—save them! They add a nice licorice flavor to tingle your palate ever so slightly once chopped and tossed over the finished dish.

—Yewande Komolafe

1½ pounds carrots, halved lengthwise if thick, cut into 3-inch pieces

1 pound yellow beets, quartered or cut into eighths if large

1 pound fennel bulbs, fronds reserved, bulbs cut into eighths

¼ cup neutral oil, such as grapeseed oil

Salt and black pepper

⅓ cup unsweetened coconut cream

1 (1-inch) piece fresh ginger, scrubbed and finely grated

1 tablespoon honey or vegan maple syrup

2 teaspoons unseasoned rice vinegar

2 teaspoons soy sauce or plant-based fish sauce

1 teaspoon Dijon mustard

1 lime

1. Heat the oven to 400 degrees.
2. On a sheet pan, drizzle the vegetables with the oil and toss to evenly coat. Season lightly with salt and pepper. Roast until vegetables are tender and golden brown, about 40 minutes.
3. Meanwhile, in a small bowl, whisk together the coconut cream, ginger, honey or maple syrup, vinegar, soy sauce and mustard. Zest the lime right into the bowl. Squeeze in 1 tablespoon lime juice and season lightly with salt and pepper. Taste the sauce and add more lime juice or salt and pepper if necessary.
4. Drizzle the dressing over the roasted vegetables while they're still hot and toss to evenly coat. Top with fennel fronds and serve warm or at room temperature.

"Amazing. Stunning, bright sauce that could be used on a number of different veg combos. Will make again."

—**Mandy**

"Fantastic hot-weather dish! I used the cuke marinade afterward as a topping on basmati rice."

—Dan

SPICY CUCUMBERS WITH YOGURT, LEMON AND HERBS

time 30 minutes

yield 4 servings

This recipe brings together two contrasting components to create a bright summer dish. A simple yogurt sauce is dressed up with herbs and zest, then topped with cucumbers that have marinated in a spicy oil. Coriander, cumin and red pepper flakes bloom in a neutral oil, and the cucumbers take on the flavors as they sit. For the yogurt, a variety of garden fresh herbs work well, but dill and mint are crucial. Both the yogurt and the cucumbers can be prepared up to a day in advance and kept refrigerated. Save a handful of the herbs for a fresh garnish.

—Yewande Komolafe

1½ pounds Persian cucumbers (about 8), quartered lengthwise and cut crosswise into 2-inch pieces

Kosher salt, such as Diamond Crystal

¼ cup grapeseed oil or other neutral oil, such as canola, safflower or sunflower oil

1 teaspoon ground coriander

½ teaspoon ground cumin

1 teaspoon red pepper flakes

2 scallions, thinly sliced

2 teaspoons apple cider vinegar

1 cup full-fat plain Greek yogurt

½ cup fresh mint leaves, thinly sliced

¼ cup chopped fresh dill

¼ cup chopped fresh parsley leaves and tender stems

1 lemon, zested and juiced

2 tablespoons olive oil

Black pepper

¼ cup toasted pine nuts (optional)

1. Toss the cucumbers with 1 teaspoon salt and set in a colander in the sink to drain.
2. In a small pot, heat the grapeseed oil over medium heat. Add the coriander and cumin and toast until fragrant, stirring to avoid scorching, about 1 minute. Remove from heat, add the red pepper flakes and let cool.
3. In a medium bowl, toss the salted cucumbers with the scallions, spiced oil and vinegar. Allow to marinate in the refrigerator for at least 15 minutes and up to overnight.
4. Meanwhile, in a small bowl, combine the yogurt, half the herbs, the lemon zest and juice and olive oil. Stir to incorporate, then season to taste with salt and pepper.
5. Spread the yogurt mixture on a plate or in the bottom of a shallow bowl. Using a slotted spoon, drain the cucumbers and scallions of excess liquid, then evenly place them on top of the yogurt. Finish with remaining chopped herbs and the pine nuts (if using) and serve immediately.

ORZO SALAD WITH LENTILS AND ZUCCHINI

VEGAN

time 40 minutes

yield 4 to 6 servings

The key to vibrant yet substantial summer salads is to mix raw and cooked ingredients and incorporate as many textures as possible. This one achieves that abundance in a streamlined manner by cooking lentils and orzo together in one pot. Start with the lentils, then add the orzo partway through cooking so both become tender at once. (You can do the same with any boiling ingredients.) The chewy orzo and velvety lentils then meet crisp, raw zucchini, crunchy nuts, and the pep of pickled peppers, scallions, lemon and a whole lot of fresh herbs—none of which requires more than a little chopping from you. Eat this protein-rich salad on its own, or add soft-boiled eggs, feta or Pecorino, as you wish.

—Ali Slagle

Kosher salt, such as Diamond Crystal

1 cup green or brown lentils

1 cup orzo

½ cup extra-virgin olive oil

¼ cup fresh lemon juice (from 2 lemons)

¼ cup sliced pickled pepperoncini (6 to 8 peppers)

Black pepper

1 pound zucchini, summer squash or a combination, preferably small to medium

⅔ cup raw pistachios or walnuts, roughly chopped

3 scallions, thinly sliced

1 cup firmly packed fresh herb leaves, such as basil, mint, dill, parsley, tarragon, oregano or a mix

1. Bring a large pot of salted water to a boil. Add the lentils and cook for 9 minutes, then add the orzo and cook until the lentils and orzo are cooked through but not mushy, another 10 to 12 minutes.
2. Meanwhile, in a large bowl, stir together the oil, lemon juice and pepperoncini. Season with ½ teaspoon each salt and black pepper. If using small or medium zucchini, halve them lengthwise, then slice crosswise into ¼-inch-thick half-moons. (If using large zucchini, quarter lengthwise, then slice crosswise into ¼-inch-thick triangles.) Add to the dressing and stir to combine.
3. Drain the lentils and orzo very well, then add to the zucchini, along with the pistachios and scallions. Stir to combine, then season to taste with salt and pepper. Stir in the herbs just before serving. Eat warm or at room temperature. Store the salad in an airtight container in the fridge for up to 4 days. Bring to room temperature and adjust seasonings before eating.

"Perfect summer salad for hot days using pantry staples."

—Lorraine

CHAPTER 3

PLATE OPTIONAL

At a passing glance, the recipes in this chapter might seem charmingly arbitrary, a bit like flipping through the menu at The Cheesecake Factory. A Vegetarian Reuben Sandwich (page 89)? Cauliflower Shawarma with Spicy Tahini (page 78)? Indian-ish Nachos with Cheddar, Black Beans and Chutney (page 82)? Surely they have nothing in common beyond how good they sound. But open your eyes and extend your hand! These are finger foods for every spirit and situation: eating straight from the pan, biting into on the go, sharing with ease or some inconceivable combination of the three.

My persistent spirit and situation: ravenous, and without a dishwasher. With a couple slices of bread, a pita or some tortillas, the plate is rendered obsolete—and so is meat. Sandwiches, burritos, shawarmas, skewers and dips are among the most gratifying (and okay, sneaky) ways to center vegetables because they provide riffable templates for cleverly and deliciously layering flavor and texture.

Savor the crunchy contrast of sweet apples and earthy walnuts against the tender and fragrant roasted vegetables in the picnic-ready Cauliflower Salad Sandwiches (page 90), made all the more delightful by their handheld nature. Do not be fooled by the charmingly petite Nashville-Style Hot Tofu Sliders (page 102)—crispy yet airy and soft inside, they pack plenty of heat and tang in a palm-size package. Behold the Crispy Mushroom Tacos (page 86), one of my house tacos for their effort-to-wow factor ratio (I recommend pressing the mushrooms beneath a smaller skillet for optimal searing). When I made them for friends a couple years back, I had to keep churning out batches; we talked as much about how tasty they were as we did about the breakup that prompted our dinner gathering.

Our readers, ever discerning, feel similarly: "Even the most die-hard meat eater would love these." Go forth and judge yourself. And while you may not need a fork or a plate, you'll certainly want a napkin or three.

CAULIFLOWER SHAWARMA WITH SPICY TAHINI
PAGE 78

ROASTED VEGETABLE BURRITOS
PAGE 81

INDIAN-ISH NACHOS WITH CHEDDAR, BLACK BEANS AND CHUTNEY
PAGE 82

CRUNCHY VEGGIE WRAPS WITH KABOCHA SQUASH
PAGE 85

CRISPY MUSHROOM TACOS
PAGE 86

VEGETARIAN REUBEN SANDWICH
PAGE 89

CAULIFLOWER SALAD SANDWICHES
PAGE 90

CHICKPEA SALAD SANDWICHES
PAGE 93

BUFFALO WHITE BEANS
PAGE 94

GRILLED MUSHROOM SKEWERS IN RED CHILE PASTE
PAGE 96

PIMENTO CHEESE AND TOMATO SANDWICHES
PAGE 99

VEGAN AL PASTOR TACOS
PAGE 100

NASHVILLE-STYLE HOT TOFU SLIDERS
PAGE 102

CAULIFLOWER SHAWARMA WITH SPICY TAHINI

VEGAN

time 45 minutes

yield 2 servings

In this vegetarian take on shawarma, the usual spiced lamb, chicken or turkey is replaced with cauliflower florets and onion wedges that have been tossed with a classic combination of cumin, paprika and coriander, then roasted until browned, fragrant and very tender. A hot sauce–spiked tahini served alongside lends creaminess and heat. To serve it, you can tuck everything into a pita or flatbread, or keep the bread on the side and let everyone assemble their own sandwiches at the table. Chopped cucumber, tomatoes and olives add a juicy brightness to contrast with the aromatic, roasted flavors.

—Melissa Clark

For the cauliflower

5 tablespoons extra-virgin olive oil, plus more as needed

1¼ teaspoons ground cumin

1¼ teaspoons sweet paprika

1 teaspoon ground coriander

¾ teaspoon fine sea salt or table salt

¼ teaspoon ground turmeric

¼ teaspoon black pepper

Pinch of ground cayenne

1 large head cauliflower (about 2½ pounds), cut into bite-size florets

1 red onion, cut into ¼-inch wedges

For the spicy tahini sauce

1 tablespoon fresh lemon juice, plus more to taste

1 teaspoon harissa paste or hot sauce, or a large pinch of Urfa or Aleppo pepper, plus more to taste

1 fat garlic clove, finely grated, passed through a press or minced

¼ teaspoon fine sea salt, plus more as needed

⅓ cup well-stirred tahini

⅓ cup ice water, plus more as needed

Pita or flatbread, for serving

¼ cup roughly chopped fresh parsley, plus more for serving

Diced tomato, cucumber and olives, for serving

1. Place racks in the upper and lower thirds of the oven and heat the oven to 425 degrees.
2. Prepare the cauliflower: In a large bowl, whisk together the oil, cumin, paprika, coriander, salt, turmeric, black pepper and cayenne. Add the cauliflower and onion and toss until well coated. Spread the mixture in a single layer on a rimmed baking sheet.
3. Roast the vegetables on the upper oven rack until golden brown, slightly crisp and tender, 30 to 40 minutes, stirring once or twice. If the vegetables look dry as they roast, drizzle with a little more oil.

4. As the vegetables cook, prepare the spicy tahini sauce: In a small bowl, whisk together the lemon juice, harissa, garlic and salt and let sit for a minute or two to mellow the garlic. Whisk in the tahini. Whisk in the ice water, 1 tablespoon at a time, until the sauce is smooth and thin enough to drizzle. You may not need all the water or you may need to add a little more: Tahini brands vary a lot. Taste and adjust seasoning, adding more harissa, lemon juice and salt if you like. The sauce should taste zippy and creamy.
5. Warm the pitas or flatbread by placing them directly on the lower oven rack during the last 5 minutes as the vegetables roast. (Or you can warm the bread on another sheet pan if that's easier for you.)
6. Scatter the parsley on top of the roasted vegetables and serve with warm pitas, tahini sauce and diced tomato, cucumber and olives.

"Huge hit with my fam. I prepared the burritos and wrapped each one in plastic wrap, then froze."

—alicia

ROASTED VEGETABLE BURRITOS

time 30 minutes

yield 4 servings

Roasted mushrooms, sweet potatoes and poblano chiles become a comforting vegetarian burrito filling in just 30 minutes. The meaty mushrooms and hearty potatoes provide substance, while the poblanos impart subtle smoky notes and mild heat. (Green bell peppers are a good nonspicy alternative.) The mashed avocado and sour cream lend creamy richness, while shredded lettuce and pico de gallo bring welcome crunch and freshness. Although not necessary, leftover rice is a nice addition to the burritos for an even more substantial meal.

—Kay Chun

12 ounces white, cremini or stuffing mushrooms, cut into ½-inch pieces

3 large poblano chiles (about 12 ounces), seeded and cut into 1-inch pieces

1 medium sweet potato (about 8 ounces), peeled and cut into ½-inch cubes

2 garlic cloves, minced

1 teaspoon dried oregano

1 teaspoon smoked paprika

¼ cup extra-virgin olive oil

Salt and black pepper

4 ounces Monterey Jack, shredded (about 1 cup)

1 ripe Hass avocado, mashed with a fork

4 (9- to 10-inch) flour tortillas

8 tablespoons sour cream

1 packed cup shredded butter or Bibb lettuce

8 tablespoons pico de gallo or salsa, store-bought or homemade

1. Heat the oven to 450 degrees. On a rimmed baking sheet, combine the mushrooms, poblanos, sweet potato, garlic, oregano, paprika and oil. Season with salt and pepper, then toss to evenly coat. Roast, stirring halfway through, until vegetables are golden and tender, about 15 minutes. Push the vegetables into a 12 by 6-inch rectangle and sprinkle with the cheese. Continue roasting just until cheese melts, about 2 minutes longer.
2. Spread one-quarter of the mashed avocado in the center of each tortilla. Top each with 2 tablespoons sour cream, ¼ cup lettuce and 2 tablespoons pico de gallo. Evenly divide the cheesy roasted vegetables among the tortillas. Fold the sides of each tortilla in over the filling; fold the bottom up and over the filling and tightly roll. Serve warm.

INDIAN-ISH NACHOS WITH CHEDDAR, BLACK BEANS AND CHUTNEY

time 30 minutes

yield 6 to 8 servings

These vegetarian nachos take their cues from papdi or papri chaat, the spicy, tangy and sweet Indian snack of fried dough wafers piled with chickpeas, tomatoes, onions, yogurt and various chutneys. This take starts with standard nacho elements: tortilla chips, black beans and a healthy amount of bubbly, melted cheese. But the classic chaat pairing of spicy and verdant cilantro chutney with sweet and sour tamarind sauce provides another level of brightness and complexity. Don't skip the chhonk, a sauce made of melted ghee, cumin seeds and red chile powder that is drizzled over the top of the nachos. It provides a rich finish and even more crunch.

—Priya Krishna and Ritu Krishna

For the cilantro chutney

1 large bunch fresh cilantro, leaves and tender stems roughly chopped (about 4 cups)

1 small Indian green chile or serrano chile, roughly chopped

2 tablespoons fresh lime juice (from about 1 lime), plus more as needed

¼ teaspoon granulated sugar

¾ teaspoon kosher salt, plus more as needed

For the nachos

1 (15-ounce) can black beans, rinsed and drained

Kosher salt, such as Diamond Crystal

1 (8-ounce) bag white corn tortilla chips, preferably unsalted

1 red onion, finely chopped

2 ripe Roma tomatoes, finely chopped

1 pound sharp Cheddar, shredded (about 4 cups)

For the chhonk

¼ cup ghee or olive oil

2 tablespoons cumin seeds

Pinch of red chile powder, such as ground cayenne

¼ cup store-bought tamarind sauce, or ¼ cup date syrup or maple syrup whisked with 1 tablespoon lime juice

Plain Greek yogurt, for serving (optional)

1. Place a rack in the top third of the oven and heat the oven to 425 degrees.
2. Prepare the chutney: In a blender, combine the cilantro, green chile, lime juice, sugar and salt and blend until smooth. If the mixture is too thick to blend, add up to 3 tablespoons water, a tablespoon at a time, to get it going. Taste and adjust the salt and lime juice, if needed. Set aside.

3. Prepare the nachos: Line a 13 by 18-inch sheet pan with foil. In a medium bowl, lightly mash the beans with a fork (this is so they won't roll off the chips) and season them with salt. Arrange half of the following on the sheet pan: the chips, beans, onion, tomatoes and cheese (in that order). Repeat to make a second layer. Bake for 7 to 10 minutes, until the cheese is melted and bubbling.
4. While the nachos are in the oven, prepare the chhonk: In a small pan or a butter warmer over medium-high, heat the ghee. Once the ghee melts (or the oil begins to shimmer), add the cumin seeds and cook until they start to sputter and brown, about 15 seconds. Immediately remove the pan from the heat and stir in the red chile powder. Set aside.
5. To serve, evenly drizzle the cilantro chutney and the tamarind sauce on top of the nachos, followed by the chhonk. Add a few dollops of the Greek yogurt (if using).

"This is such a great recipe for make-ahead lunches!"

—**Michaela H.**

CRUNCHY VEGGIE WRAPS WITH KABOCHA SQUASH

VEGAN

time 50 minutes

yield 6 wraps

Kabocha, spiced with coriander, cumin and paprika, is the star of these vegetable wraps. The salad that is added to the wraps is crunchy and satisfying—and so delicious you might want to skip the wrap aspect and let the salad shine. If you want to turn these handheld sandwiches into plated salads, feel free to simply add a little more lettuce to the herb salad mix and top it with the roasted squash. Every component of this dish is great for meal prep; for best results, keep them separate before assembling.

—Sue Li

1 teaspoon ground coriander

1 teaspoon ground cumin

1 teaspoon smoked paprika

Kosher salt and black pepper

3 tablespoons olive oil

1½ pounds kabocha squash (from ½ small kabocha squash), sliced into ½-inch-thick wedges

½ red onion, thinly sliced

¼ cup vegan (or regular) mayonnaise

1 garlic clove, grated

1 tablespoon fresh lemon juice

3 Persian cucumbers, thinly sliced

1½ cups cilantro leaves and tender stems

1½ cups mint leaves

2 cups roughly chopped romaine lettuce

6 large whole wheat tortillas or a wrap of your choice

1 pint alfalfa sprouts

1. Heat the oven to 400 degrees. Combine the coriander, cumin, paprika, 1½ teaspoons salt, ½ teaspoon pepper and the oil in a small bowl. On a baking sheet, toss the squash with the spice mixture using your hands. Arrange the squash in a single layer and roast until tender and lightly golden at the edges, 20 to 22 minutes, tossing halfway through. Remove from the oven and let cool.
2. While the squash roasts, soak the onion in cold water for about 5 minutes. Drain and set aside.
3. While the squash roasts, make the dressing: In a large bowl whisk together the mayonnaise, garlic and lemon juice. Season with salt.
4. To assemble the wraps, toss the cucumbers, cilantro, mint, lettuce and onion in the dressing, then divide among the tortillas. Top with the roasted squash and then alfalfa sprouts.
5. To roll the wraps, fold the bottom of each tortilla over the filling. Fold in the sides, then roll up tightly. Cut the wraps in half, if desired. (If making in advance, store the greens, dressing and squash separately until ready to assemble.)

CRISPY MUSHROOM TACOS

VEGAN

time 40 minutes

yield 4 servings

This simple recipe calls for pan-searing meaty oyster mushrooms so they become as perfectly crispy and golden as chicharrón. Paired with fresh pico de gallo, these mushrooms feel satisfying with their natural umami savoriness. This quick dish tastes like juicy *carnicería* tacos that balance the richness of fried meat with the acidic punch of salsa.

—Jocelyn Ramirez

For the avocado pico de gallo

1 large beefsteak tomato, cut into ¼-inch dice

1 large ripe Hass avocado, cut into ¼-inch dice

2 jalapeños, finely chopped (seeded, if desired)

½ cup cilantro leaves, finely chopped

3 tablespoons fresh lime juice (from 1 to 2 limes)

Coarse kosher salt

For the mushroom tacos

1½ pounds oyster mushrooms (from 2 to 3 medium clusters)

⅓ cup neutral oil, such as canola oil

¼ teaspoon ground cumin

1½ teaspoons coarse kosher salt

Black pepper

12 corn tortillas

1. Prepare the avocado pico de gallo: In a small bowl, combine the tomato, avocado, jalapeños, cilantro and lime juice and season with salt. Gently fold together. Set aside to allow flavors to marry while the mushrooms cook.
2. Prepare the tacos: Tear the oyster mushrooms into bite-size pieces, leaving some whole. To make sure the mushrooms become crisp, cook in two batches: In a large cast-iron or other heavy skillet, heat half the oil over medium-high heat. Add half the mushrooms in a single layer without crowding the skillet. Cook, stirring every few minutes, until deep golden brown and crisp, 10 to 15 minutes. Transfer to a plate, then repeat with the remaining oil and mushrooms. Return the first batch of mushrooms to the skillet, add the cumin and salt, and season with pepper. Stir well, then remove from the heat.
3. While the mushrooms are cooking, on a comal or in another large heavy skillet, warm the tortillas over medium-high heat until soft and pliable. Wrap them in a dish towel to keep warm until ready to serve. Divide the mushrooms and pico de gallo among the warm tortillas. Serve immediately.

"This is shockingly good! Even the most die-hard meat eater would love these. So easy and so delicious with great depth of flavor."

—Sarah

"I've made this several times and this is the bomb. I may or may not double up on the Swiss, I'll let you all decide for yourselves."

—Julia

VEGETARIAN REUBEN SANDWICH

time 15 minutes

yield 1 sandwich

The Reuben sandwich—corned beef, sauerkraut, Swiss cheese and Russian dressing on rye bread—has inspired many meat-free versions. Tempeh, seitan, vegetables and mushrooms have stood in for the corned beef, but they're not really needed, because outsize quantities of the other traditional elements make a punchy, gooey sandwich on their own. Both sides of the buttered rye get melted Swiss, and the mountain of sauerkraut doesn't warm long enough to lose its crunch. The specks of pickles and onion in typical Russian dressing become layers in the sandwich. And while the dressing has mayonnaise and ketchup, as usual, it also has coriander and black pepper to evoke corned beef's brine, plus hot sauce for kick. Because this rejiggered sandwich relies mostly on condiments and pantry staples, this homemade Reuben is within reach any day.

—Ali Slagle

1 tablespoon mayonnaise

1 tablespoon ketchup

½ teaspoon hot sauce, or to taste

¼ teaspoon ground coriander

Salt and black pepper

2 slices rye bread

2 slices Swiss cheese

½ tablespoon unsalted butter

¼ cup thinly sliced white onion or shallot

½ cup very well drained and squeezed sauerkraut

1 dill pickle, sliced, or 2 dill pickle sandwich slices

1. In a small bowl, stir together the mayonnaise, ketchup, hot sauce and coriander. Season with salt and pepper. Taste and adjust the pepper and hot sauce until the dressing is just a bit too intense, as it will be tamed by the sandwich fillings.
2. Spread the dressing on both slices of bread. Reserve the bowl and any remaining dressing. Top each bread slice with a slice of Swiss cheese. In a large skillet with a lid, melt the butter over medium-low heat. Add the bread, cheese side up. Swirl the bread slices around the skillet to mop up the butter. Cover the skillet and cook until the cheese is melted and the bread is golden, 4 to 5 minutes. Meanwhile, place the onion and a pinch of salt in the reserved bowl and stir to coat in the residual dressing.
3. Top one slice of bread with the sauerkraut, pickles and onions. Flip the other slice onto the fillings and press lightly to adhere. Cook for just a minute on each side until the sandwich has sealed. Slice and eat warm.

CAULIFLOWER SALAD SANDWICHES

time 30 minutes

yield 4 sandwiches

Pulling from the greatest hits of chicken salads, with crunchy walnuts, crisp apples, sweet raisins and a spiced mayo-yogurt dressing, this best-of-all-worlds sandwich swaps out the chicken for cauliflower. The aggressively roasted cauliflower serves as a sponge, soaking up all the flavors of the dressing while adding layers of bitterness and earthiness. The salad only gets better as it sits, allowing the flavors to meld and the cauliflower to soak up even more dressing. Even after it's built, the sandwich improves as it sits for a few hours. Do you plan ahead? This makes an ideal picnic dish. Not sure when you'll get a chance to eat or where the day will take you? This is here for you.

—Ham El-Waylly

1 large head cauliflower (about 2 pounds), halved and cut into 1-inch slices

6 tablespoons neutral oil

5 teaspoons curry powder

Salt

1 cup raw walnuts, roughly chopped

1 tart, crisp apple, chopped into ½-inch pieces

1 lemon, zested and juiced, plus more to taste

½ cup mayonnaise

½ cup strained yogurt, like Greek or skyr

⅓ cup raisins

½ cup cilantro leaves and tender stems, roughly chopped

½ cup parsley leaves, roughly chopped

4 hoagie rolls, split lengthwise

1. Place a large, rimmed baking sheet on the middle rack of the oven and heat the oven to 450 degrees.
2. In a large bowl, toss the cauliflower with 3 tablespoons oil, 2 teaspoons curry powder and a large pinch of salt. Massage the cauliflower to separate it into individual florets and coat it evenly in oil. Carefully spread the cauliflower out on the hot baking sheet and roast until cooked through and charred in spots, about 20 minutes. Turn the broiler on high and cook until cauliflower is deep brown and well charred, 3 to 5 minutes.
3. While the cauliflower roasts, toast the walnuts: In a small skillet, heat remaining 3 tablespoons oil over medium heat, add the walnuts and a pinch of salt and cook, stirring frequently, until lightly toasted, 3 to 4 minutes. Stir in remaining 3 teaspoons curry powder, turn off heat and cook until fragrant, about 1 minute.
4. In a large bowl, stir together the apple, lemon zest and juice, and a large pinch of salt. Add the mayonnaise, yogurt, raisins, cilantro, parsley and the walnut mixture, taking care to scrape in all the oil and curry, and stir to combine.

"A friend brought this to a potluck and it was divine, so I brought it to a potluck and it disappeared."

—**Seagreen**

5. Add the cauliflower and toss until well combined. Season with salt to taste. The cauliflower salad will keep in an airtight container in the fridge for up to 3 days.
6. Divide the cauliflower salad among the rolls and press firmly to close. Eat sandwiches immediately or within 12 hours; refrigerate after an hour.

"I can't make this often enough. The chickpea foundation is like a palette waiting for different paints . . . Bon appétit and be bold."

—Robert

CHICKPEA SALAD SANDWICHES

time 10 minutes

yield 4 sandwiches

This quick recipe transforms simple canned chickpeas into a bold and hearty vegetarian meal. Chickpeas are mashed in a creamy, rich lemon-tahini dressing, then mixed with crunchy celery and scallions for fresh bite. Earthy alfalfa sprouts, crisp lettuce, creamy avocado and sweet tomatoes bring contrasting textures and flavors to the sandwich. The chickpea salad can be made a few hours ahead and kept refrigerated. Any leftover salad makes a tasty dip served with tortilla chips or crackers. For a vegan alternative, use a vegan mayonnaise and omit the cheese for sandwiches that still boast layers of flavor.

—Kay Chun

6 tablespoons extra-virgin olive oil

6 tablespoons well-stirred tahini

3 tablespoons fresh lemon juice (from 1 large lemon)

½ teaspoon grated garlic

Salt and black pepper

2 (15-ounce) cans chickpeas, rinsed and drained

½ cup finely chopped celery

½ cup finely chopped scallions

½ cup freshly grated Parmesan

8 slices multigrain sandwich bread

Mayonnaise, for spreading

8 butter lettuce leaves

1 (packed) cup alfalfa sprouts

1 Hass avocado, thinly sliced

1 large ripe tomato, thinly sliced

1. In a large bowl, combine the oil, tahini, lemon juice and garlic. Season with salt and pepper, then whisk until well combined. Add the chickpeas and mash with the back of a fork or spoon until chunky. Add the celery, scallions and cheese and mix well. Season with salt and pepper.
2. Spread each slice of bread with mayonnaise. Divide the lettuce, alfalfa and avocado among 4 of the slices, then top with some of the chickpea salad and tomatoes. Close sandwiches and serve. (Sandwiches may sit at room temperature for 1 to 2 hours before serving.)

BUFFALO WHITE BEANS

time 20 minutes

yield 3 to 4 servings

This spicy-tangy vegetarian skillet comes together quickly, helped along by pantry ingredients and a few hardy vegetables. Don't skimp on the butter! Classic Buffalo flavor depends not only on the vinegary hot sauce but also a rich butter base. Celery leaves make a fresh herbal topping; if your stalks don't have leaves, grab some extras from the middle of the bunch. Eat these beans with a spoon straight from the pan, scoop them up with chips or tuck them into tortillas.

—Sarah DiGregorio

¼ cup unsalted butter

2 celery stalks, finely chopped, leaves reserved

2 medium carrots, finely chopped

¼ teaspoon coarse kosher salt

6 large garlic cloves, smashed and chopped

2 (15-ounce) cans cannellini beans, rinsed and drained

¼ cup Buffalo-style hot sauce, such as Frank's RedHot, plus more for serving

Black pepper

½ cup panko bread crumbs

⅓ cup crumbled blue cheese

1. Heat the oven to 475 degrees. Place an oven-safe 10-inch skillet over medium-high heat and melt the butter. Add the celery, carrots and salt and cook, stirring occasionally, until softened, about 5 minutes. Add the garlic and cook, stirring occasionally, until softened, for 1 minute. Add the beans, hot sauce, and several generous grinds of black pepper. Stir to combine. Turn off the heat. Sprinkle the panko evenly over the beans, then the blue cheese crumbles.
2. Bake until the panko is crisp and toasted and the blue cheese has softened, 8 to 10 minutes. Top with celery leaves and serve with more hot sauce as needed.

"Served as a hot dip
and it was a huge hit."

—**K. Army**

GRILLED MUSHROOM SKEWERS IN RED CHILE PASTE

VEGAN

time 45 minutes

yield 4 to 6 servings

Fire up the grill and let the aromas of vegetables and chile-marinated mushrooms charred over an open flame permeate the neighborhood. This simple recipe is fun to assemble, and a crowd pleaser, making it ideal for cookouts. Meaty king oyster mushrooms are smothered in a guajillo chile sauce that includes earthy achiote, which stains the mushrooms red. Liquid aminos or soy sauce add saltiness and umami, and maple syrup brings a touch of sweetness.

—Jocelyn Ramirez

12 bamboo skewers (about 8 inches long)

4 medium guajillo chiles, seeded and rinsed

2 garlic cloves

Salt and black pepper

2 large yellow or orange bell peppers, cut into 1-inch dice

2 large zucchini, cut into ½-inch-thick coins

10 ounces cherry tomatoes (about 20)

¼ cup plus 1 tablespoon neutral oil, plus more if needed

1 tablespoon achiote paste (see Tip)

1 tablespoon liquid aminos or soy sauce

1½ teaspoons pure maple syrup

½ teaspoon ground cumin

12 ounces king oyster mushrooms (about 10)

1 lemon, halved

Flaky sea salt, for garnish

1. If cooking outdoors, prepare a charcoal grill or heat a gas grill to medium-high. Soak the bamboo skewers in cold water for at least 30 minutes.
2. In a small saucepan with a lid, bring 1 cup water to a boil over high heat. Add the chiles, garlic and a pinch of salt. Cover partially, reduce heat to medium-low and simmer until the chiles have rehydrated and the garlic has softened, about 10 minutes.
3. While the chile mixture simmers, in a large bowl toss the bell peppers, zucchini and tomatoes with 1 tablespoon oil and season with salt and pepper.
4. Using a slotted spoon, transfer the rehydrated chiles and softened garlic to a blender or food processor along with ½ cup of the cooking liquid. Add the achiote paste, liquid aminos, maple syrup, cumin and remaining ¼ cup oil, and blend until completely smooth. Transfer to a large bowl.
5. Cut off the mushroom caps and cut the stems into ½-inch-thick coins. Halve or quarter the caps. Add the mushrooms to the chile paste and mix until coated.

Tip

Achiote or annatto seeds have an earthy, floral and slightly bitter flavor. They're used both for seasoning and as a natural food coloring. Achiote paste is made by grinding the seeds with garlic, chiles and other spices and can be purchased at most supermarkets, Mexican grocery stores or online.

"Makes killer vegan tacos. Corn tortillas and some avocado or guacamole."

—AWW

6. To assemble, load the vegetables onto all the skewers. Start and end each skewer with a piece of bell pepper and alternate among the mushroom slices, bell peppers, zucchini coins and tomatoes in between, going heavy on the mushrooms. Brush any remaining paste over the mushrooms.
7. If cooking outdoors, set the skewers on the hot grill grate. If cooking indoors, turn gas burners to medium-high heat or heat a griddle or grill pan on an electric or induction stovetop over medium-high heat. If using a gas range, cook the skewers directly on the grates over the open flame. If using a griddle or pan, set the skewers on the hot surface. Cook until slightly charred and fragrant, turning occasionally with tongs to grill evenly, about 15 minutes. Grill the lemon halves until charred, if you like.
8. Transfer the skewers to a serving dish and finish with a squeeze of lemon juice and a pinch of flaky salt. Serve immediately.

"This sandwich is easy and satisfying. Don't judge me, but I put on arugula."

—**Barbara**

PIMENTO CHEESE AND TOMATO SANDWICHES

time 25 minutes

yield 8 sandwiches

Every summer, Southerners await the arrival of juicy, ripe tomatoes to make a classic tomato sandwich. This version of the beloved staple swaps pimento cheese for mayonnaise as the creamy companion. The spread is studded with sharp Cheddar and jalapeño, giving it just enough kick without completely overshadowing the tomato. Choose tomatoes that are ripe but still somewhat firm: You want them to have enough structural integrity to prevent a soggy sandwich. While many Southerners prefer plain white bread, you could opt for sourdough or brioche. This recipe is great for parties and group picnics, but don't feel pressured to make these only for a crowd—the recipe can easily be halved. You could also use the extra pimento cheese to spread on crackers or add to biscuit dough. You'll end up with four cups of it, which will keep in the refrigerator for up to a week. The sandwiches, however, are best eaten as soon as they're assembled.

—Kia Damon

8 ounces cream cheese, softened

8 ounces sharp Cheddar, grated (about 2 cups)

½ cup mayonnaise

1 (8-ounce) jar pimentos, drained and minced (about 1½ cups)

1 jalapeño, seeded and diced

1 teaspoon dry mustard

1 teaspoon paprika

½ teaspoon ground cayenne

Salt

2 large heirloom tomatoes (preferably ripe but firm)

16 slices white bread

1. Mix the cheeses, mayonnaise, pimentos, jalapeño, mustard powder, paprika and cayenne in a large bowl until thoroughly combined. Season with salt to taste. Cut the tomatoes crosswise into ½-inch-thick slices. Toast the bread.
2. To assemble each sandwich, spread ¼ cup pimento cheese on each slice of bread, add a slice of tomato to one side, sprinkle lightly with salt and close the sandwich. Slice into your preferred shape and eat immediately.

VEGAN TACOS AL PASTOR

VEGAN

time 35 minutes

yield 4 servings

Inspired by tacos al pastor, this peppy vegan version gives a firm nod to the smoky, savory and sweet flavors of the famed Mexican street food. The shortcut adobo (marinade) forgoes dried Mexican chiles and instead uses canned chipotle chiles in adobo sauce, as well as fresh pineapple and additional spices. While the inclusion of soy sauce may be unconventional here, tempeh has a mild flavor that benefits from aggressive seasoning and the extra injection of umami. Pineapple, a signature ingredient of al pastor, is used two ways, adding sweetness to both the spiced marinade and the bold salsa.

—Hetty Lui McKinnon

For the tempeh

2 to 3 canned chipotle chiles in adobo, plus 2 to 3 tablespoons adobo sauce (to your liking)

2 teaspoons ground cumin

2 teaspoons smoked paprika

2 garlic cloves, roughly chopped

2 ounces fresh pineapple, cut into ½-inch chunks (about ⅓ cup)

5 tablespoons extra-virgin olive oil, plus more as needed

2 tablespoons soy sauce

2 (8-ounce) blocks tempeh, crumbled

Salt and black pepper

For the pineapple and jalapeño salsa

6 ounces fresh pineapple, finely chopped (about 1 cup)

½ to 1 jalapeño (to your liking), finely chopped

½ cup chopped fresh cilantro leaves and tender stems

Juice of ½ to 1 lime, to taste

Salt

8 to 12 (6-inch) corn tortillas, warmed

1 lime, cut into quarters

1. Prepare the tempeh: Place the chipotle chiles, adobo sauce, cumin, paprika, garlic, pineapple, 3 tablespoons olive oil and soy sauce in a small blender or food processor and blend until smooth.
2. Transfer the marinade to a large bowl and add the tempeh; season generously with salt and pepper and toss to coat.
3. Heat a large skillet over medium-high. When the pan is hot, drizzle with remaining 2 tablespoons olive oil, add the tempeh mixture and flatten into a single layer, ensuring as much of the tempeh is in contact with the hot surface of the pan as possible. Cook undisturbed until charred on the bottom, 2 to 3 minutes. Toss and cook undisturbed again for another 2 minutes. Repeat once more, until the tempeh is mostly charred. If the tempeh seems dry at any point, add some

"Loved this! Served it with a side of roasted new potatoes, poblano and red onion."

—Erin

more olive oil. Taste the tempeh to make sure you are happy with the seasoning, adding more salt if needed.

4. Make the salsa: In a medium bowl, toss the pineapple, jalapeño, cilantro and lime juice to combine. Season to taste with salt.
5. To serve, top each tortilla with tempeh and some salsa. Serve with lime wedges on the side.

NASHVILLE-STYLE HOT TOFU SLIDERS

time 30 minutes

yield 4 servings

Nashville hot chicken is seasoned with a bold dose of ground cayenne and hot sauce, deep fried and then brushed with a final coat of spicy oil. In these vegetarian sliders, hot butter imbues mild tofu with an extra-spicy kick reminiscent of the chicken that inspired them. Tofu has a high water content, but a quick dredge in rice flour and a dip in batter creates a barrier that prevents excessive splattering during frying. The carbonation in the seltzer keeps the batter light and airy, perfect for delicate tofu. The result is a golden sandwich filling with a crispy exterior and a soft center. For larger sandwiches, stuff standard hamburger buns with two pieces of the fried tofu and finish with the toppings.

—Kay Chun

For the hot butter

8 tablespoons unsalted butter, melted

2 tablespoons distilled white vinegar

1 tablespoon Louisiana-style hot sauce, such as Tabasco

1 tablespoon ground cayenne

1 teaspoon black pepper

½ teaspoon garlic powder

½ teaspoon onion powder

For the tofu

1 (14- to 16-ounce) package firm tofu, drained

¼ cup whole milk

½ cup white rice flour

½ cup all-purpose flour

2 tablespoons cornstarch

2 teaspoons baking powder

Salt

½ cup plus 2 tablespoons chilled seltzer or club soda

Vegetable oil, for shallow frying

For assembly

Mayonnaise, for spreading

8 slider buns, or 4 slices white bread

Lettuce, such as iceberg or butter

Sliced dill pickles

1. Prepare the hot butter: In a small bowl, combine all the ingredients and whisk until well blended. Set aside.
2. Prepare the tofu: Line a plate with paper towels. With a hand on top of the tofu, cut parallel to the cutting board so that you have 2 equal rectangles. Quarter each of those rectangles, so that you have 8 pieces. Arrange on the prepared plate and top with another layer of paper towels. Press to remove excess water.
3. Place the milk and rice flour in separate shallow bowls. In a medium bowl, whisk the all-purpose flour, cornstarch and baking powder. Season with salt, then add the seltzer and gently whisk just to combine. Do not overmix—a few lumps in the batter are okay.

"A delicious next-level way to eat fried tofu!"

—Therese

4. Line another plate with paper towels. In a large cast-iron skillet, heat ½ inch oil over medium heat to 375 degrees. Working with 4 pieces of the tofu at a time, dredge in milk, then in rice flour, pressing all sides of the tofu into the rice flour. The tofu should be completely coated with flour. Dip in the batter, allowing excess to drip off, then carefully place in the hot skillet. Fry undisturbed until batter sets, about 2 minutes. Flip gently and continue to fry until golden and crisp, about 3 minutes longer, adjusting heat as necessary to stay close to 375 degrees. Transfer to prepared plate and season with salt. Repeat dredging and frying with the remaining tofu.
5. To assemble: Spread mayonnaise on the cut sides of the buns. (If using sliced bread, cut into quarters for slider-size portions.) Arrange lettuce on bottom buns. Gently turn each piece of tofu in the hot butter to evenly coat, then place on top of lettuce. Drizzle with more hot butter, top with pickles and finish with bun tops. Serve warm.

CHAPTER 4

SOUP WEATHER

When I was a kid, the surest sign of the holidays was the appearance of an industrial-size stockpot on the stove. Christmas meant a metric ton of borscht, ruby and inviting. It remains my favorite part of the season, so much so that I often kick things off by making my first pot of the stuff . . . on Halloween. For many, soup is a dish of pragmatism. But for me, it has always been one of celebration: that first pitcher of gazpacho to mark summer's peak, the bowl of warming potato soup that heralds *When Harry Met Sally* season.

The real broth buffs will need little convincing to turn the page. But I know what the spoon-averse are thinking. "Soup isn't filling." "Soup is too one-note." "If I wanted to drink my dinner, I'd have a smoothie. Or better yet, a martini." The recipes in this chapter have the capacity to convert. They are fortifying and filling, like Naz Deravian's White Bean, Rice and Dill Soup (page 127), a sparkling sum so much greater than its pantry and crisper parts. And they're varied in their textures, like Yewande Komolafe's Asaro (Yam and Plantain Curry, page 118), bobbing with soft tubers and topped with crunchy shallots and fresh herbs.

Short of a salad, soup might be the easiest way to bring together a motley of vegetables, legumes and grains that, in the end, feels cohesive, intentional and, most important, satisfying. And if you, like me, loathe throwing away slightly wilted produce, soup is your savior.

A good soup often starts with a better base, like Ali Slagle's Vegetable Stock (page 224), for which you can simply raid your crisper scraps—leeks, scallions, celery, celery root, tomatoes, fennel, parsnips, corn, (breathe) and carrots, plus all their stems and leaves and roots. But many of the delectable soups ahead start, as life does, with water: Samin Nosrat's Butternut Squash and Green Curry Soup (page 124); Melissa Clark's Lemony Carrot and Cauliflower Soup (page 114); Hetty Lui McKinnon's Broccoli-Quinoa Soup with Turmeric and Ginger (page 132). Four, five, six cups of water, and you're on your way to something worth celebrating.

CREAMY CAULIFLOWER SOUP WITH ROSEMARY OLIVE OIL
PAGE 106

GOLDEN POTATO AND GREENS SOUP
PAGE 109

CABBAGE AND PARMESAN SOUP
PAGE 110

RED LENTIL SOUP
PAGE 113

LEMONY CARROT AND CAULIFLOWER SOUP
PAGE 114

LEMONY PEARL BARLEY SOUP
PAGE 117

ASARO (YAM AND PLANTAIN CURRY)
PAGE 118

GOCHUJANG POTATO STEW
PAGE 120

SPRING MINESTRONE WITH KALE AND PASTA
PAGE 123

BUTTERNUT SQUASH AND GREEN CURRY SOUP
PAGE 124

WHITE BEAN, RICE AND DILL SOUP
PAGE 127

SOMEN NOODLE SOUP WITH MUSHROOMS
PAGE 128

COCONUT BLACK BEAN SOUP
PAGE 131

BROCCOLI-QUINOA SOUP WITH TURMERIC AND GINGER
PAGE 132

BROTHY THAI CURRY WITH SILKEN TOFU AND HERBS
PAGE 135

CREAMY CAULIFLOWER SOUP WITH ROSEMARY OLIVE OIL

VEGAN

time 40 minutes

yield 6 servings

This soup turns a short list of vegan ingredients into a sublimely silky soup. Infusing olive oil with fresh rosemary is a trick you'll want to keep up your sleeve: The results are delicious drizzled over roasted winter vegetables or even just sopped up with a nice piece of bread. The croutons here are optional, but they transform an elegant and delicate first-course soup into a satisfying lunch.

—Lidey Heuck

For the rosemary oil

1 cup olive oil

4 (4-inch) rosemary sprigs

For the soup

2 tablespoons olive oil

1 yellow onion, chopped (about 1 cup)

2 garlic cloves, minced

1 quart low-sodium vegetable stock, store-bought or homemade (page 224), plus more as needed for reheating

1 large head cauliflower (about 2½ pounds), cut into 1½-inch florets

2 teaspoons kosher salt, such as Diamond Crystal, plus more to taste

1 teaspoon black pepper, plus more to taste

1 lemon, zested

For the croutons (optional)

3 cups ¾-inch-diced rustic country bread

Kosher salt and black pepper

1. Prepare the rosemary oil: In a medium skillet, combine the oil and rosemary sprigs and cook over low heat for 5 minutes, reducing the heat if the oil reaches a full simmer. (You want to cook at a very gentle simmer to avoid frying the rosemary.) Carefully pour the oil and rosemary into a small bowl, leaving a slick of oil in the pan if you plan to make croutons. Allow the rosemary to cool completely in the oil while you make the soup.
2. Prepare the soup: In a large Dutch oven or other heavy pot with a lid, heat the oil over medium-low heat. Add the onion and cook, stirring occasionally, until tender and translucent, 6 to 8 minutes. Add the garlic and cook until fragrant, about 30 seconds. (Be careful not to let the garlic scorch!)
3. Add the stock, cauliflower, salt and pepper, and bring to a boil over high heat. Reduce heat to low, cover, and simmer until the cauliflower is tender when pierced with a fork, about 10 minutes.
4. Meanwhile, prepare the optional croutons: Heat the reserved skillet with the residual rosemary oil over medium heat. Add the bread cubes, sprinkle generously with salt and pepper, and cook, tossing often, until toasted all over, 4 to 5 minutes. Transfer the croutons to a plate or board to cool.

5. Strain and discard the rosemary stems from the rosemary oil. Working in batches if necessary, carefully transfer the vegetables, stock and ¼ cup rosemary oil to a blender and blend on high until creamy. Add more rosemary oil to taste, and blend to combine. Return the soup to the pot and bring to a simmer. If the soup seems thin, let it simmer for 5 to 10 minutes to reduce slightly. (Remember: The soup will continue to thicken as it cools.) Season to taste with salt and pepper.
6. Serve hot. Garnish each serving with a swirl of rosemary oil, some croutons, and a sprinkle of lemon zest. The soup will thicken as it sits; add more stock as necessary when reheating. Leftover rosemary oil will keep in an airtight container at room temperature for up to 1 week. Store any leftover croutons in an airtight container at room temperature for up to 5 days.

"Rustic, nourishing and mouth-wateringly delicious."

—Diya

GOLDEN POTATO AND GREENS SOUP

VEGAN

time 1 hour

yield 4 to 6 servings

This very creamy take on potato-leek soup didn't set out to be vegan—it just happened along the way. The secret to its luxurious texture is not dairy but rather mashing the potatoes in the soup pot as they soften, which releases their thickening starches, no blender necessary. (That said, you can certainly add cream if desired.) Hearty greens like Swiss chard or kale make the soup more filling, and ground turmeric imparts a wonderful golden color. If you want to freeze the soup, simply leave out the greens and add them when it's time to reheat.

—Andy Baraghani

¼ cup extra-virgin olive oil, plus more for garnish

2 medium leeks, white and green parts, finely chopped

4 garlic cloves, thinly sliced

2 pounds baby Yukon Gold potatoes, sliced into rounds (about ¼ inch thick)

2 teaspoons ground turmeric

1 teaspoon red pepper flakes

Salt and black pepper

1 bunch Swiss chard, kale or mature spinach, stems removed, leaves roughly chopped

Chopped fresh dill, for garnish

1. Heat the oil in a large pot over medium-high. Add the leeks and garlic and cook, stirring occasionally, until the leeks are softened but not browned, 4 to 6 minutes. Add the potatoes, turmeric and red pepper flakes and season with salt and black pepper. Using a wooden spoon, give the potatoes and leeks a good stir to coat with the spices.
2. Pour in 5 cups water, season with more salt and bring to a simmer. Cook, stirring occasionally, until the potatoes are very soft and nearly falling apart, 25 to 30 minutes. Use the spoon to mash a few of the potatoes to help them release their starch, which will thicken the soup and make it even more creamy. Throw in the Swiss chard and simmer until just wilted, 2 to 3 minutes. Taste and add more salt if needed.
3. Ladle the soup into bowls. Scatter dill over the top, drizzle with oil and finish with a few cranks of black pepper.

CABBAGE AND PARMESAN SOUP

time 55 minutes

yield 4 to 6 servings

This warming, nourishing soup, thickened with rice, is full of soft strands of green cabbage. Parmesan is used here in two ways: The rinds are simmered with the stock, and the cheese is grated and sprinkled on top, adding complexity and body. If you like a kick, you can increase the red pepper flakes, or leave them out entirely for a supremely gentle broth. Add a squeeze of lemon right at the end if you like your soup on the tart side.

—Melissa Clark

2 tablespoons unsalted butter

2 medium leeks, white and light green parts only, halved lengthwise and thinly sliced

3 garlic cloves, minced or finely grated

⅛ teaspoon red pepper flakes, plus more for serving (optional)

1 small head green cabbage (about 1¼ pounds), roughly chopped (about 9 cups)

1½ teaspoons fine sea salt or kosher salt, plus more to taste

½ teaspoon freshly ground black pepper, plus more to taste

2 quarts vegetable stock, store-bought or homemade (page 224)

1 cup long-grain rice

5 thyme sprigs

2 Parmesan rinds, or 2 tablespoons of another grated cheese

1 lemon

¼ cup grated Parmesan, plus more for serving

1 cup chopped fresh dill or cilantro, or a combination

1. In a Dutch oven or other heavy pot with a lid, melt the butter over medium-high heat. Add the leeks and cook, stirring occasionally, until soft and lightly golden, 5 to 7 minutes. Stir in the garlic and red pepper flakes (if using) and cook until fragrant, about 1 minute. Add the cabbage, salt and pepper and cook until the cabbage wilts slightly and begins to caramelize, about 10 minutes.
2. Stir in the stock, rice and thyme. If using the Parmesan rinds, add them now and bring everything to a simmer. Cook, partly covered, over medium-low heat until cabbage and rice are very tender, 20 to 25 minutes.
3. Discard the thyme sprigs and Parmesan rinds. Using a Microplane or other fine grater, grate in the zest from the lemon. Stir in the grated Parmesan and dill.
4. Halve the lemon and squeeze in the juice from one of the halves. Cut the remaining lemon half into wedges for serving. Taste the soup and add more salt and pepper, if needed. To serve, ladle into soup bowls and garnish with more grated cheese, a lemon wedge and more red pepper flakes, if you like.

"This recipe is perfect for driving the winter blues away!"

—**Mithila**

"This soup is so tasty and good, it's hard to believe how easy it is to make. Bright, delicious flavors!"

—Doren

RED LENTIL SOUP

VEGAN

time 45 minutes

yield 4 servings

This is a lentil soup that defies expectations. Based on the Turkish lentil soup mercimek corbasi, it is light, spicy and a bold red in color (no murky brown here): a revelatory dish that takes less than an hour to make. The cooking is painless. Sauté onion and garlic in oil, then stir in tomato paste, cumin and chile powder and cook a few minutes more to intensify flavor. Add the broth, water, red lentils (which cook faster than their green or black counterparts) and diced carrot, and simmer for 30 minutes. Purée half the mixture and return it to the pot for a soup that strikes a balance between chunky and pleasingly smooth. A hit of lemon juice adds a top note that offsets the deep cumin and chile flavors.

—Melissa Clark

3 tablespoons olive oil, plus more for drizzling

1 large onion, chopped

2 garlic cloves, minced

1 tablespoon tomato paste

1 teaspoon ground cumin

¼ teaspoon fine sea salt, plus more to taste

¼ teaspoon black pepper

Pinch of chile powder or ground cayenne, plus more for serving

1 quart vegetable broth, store-bought or homemade (page 224)

1 cup red lentils

1 large carrot, diced

Juice of ½ lemon, plus more for serving

3 tablespoons chopped fresh cilantro

1. In a large Dutch oven or other heavy pot with a lid, heat the oil over high heat until hot and shimmering. Add the onion and garlic and sauté until golden, about 4 minutes.
2. Stir in the tomato paste, cumin, salt, black pepper and chile powder and sauté for 2 minutes longer.
3. Add the broth, 2 cups water, the lentils and carrot. Bring to a simmer, then partly cover the pot and turn heat to medium-low. Simmer until the lentils are soft, about 30 minutes. Taste and add salt if necessary.
4. Using an immersion or regular blender or a food processor, purée half the soup, then add it back to pot. The soup should be somewhat chunky.
5. Reheat the soup, if necessary, then stir in the lemon juice and cilantro. Serve the soup drizzled with olive oil and dusted lightly with chile powder, if desired.

LEMONY CARROT AND CAULIFLOWER SOUP

VEGAN

time 40 minutes

yield 4 servings

The beauty of a soup like this—other than its bone-warming properties—is that you don't need a recipe. You can pretty much simmer together any combination of vegetables with a little water or broth, purée it, top it with olive oil and season with salt and end up with something good to eat. The addition of miso paste and crushed coriander to the broth, and fresh lemon and cilantro at the end, zips things up without negating the comfort factor.

—Melissa Clark

1 tablespoon coriander seeds

2 tablespoons extra-virgin olive oil, plus more for serving

1 white onion, diced (about 2 cups)

2 large garlic cloves, finely chopped

5 medium carrots (1 pound), cut into ½-inch pieces (about 2 cups)

1½ teaspoons kosher salt, such as Diamond Crystal, plus more as needed

3 tablespoons white miso paste

1 small or ½ large head cauliflower (1 to 1½ pounds), cut into florets

½ teaspoon lemon zest

2 tablespoons fresh lemon juice

Smoky chile powder, for serving

Coarse sea salt, for serving

Cilantro leaves, for serving

1. In a large, dry pot with a lid, toast the coriander seeds over medium heat until fragrant and dark golden brown, 2 to 3 minutes. Transfer to a mortar and coarsely crush with the pestle.
2. Return the pot to medium heat. Add the oil and heat until warm. Add the onion and cook, stirring occasionally, until soft and lightly colored, 7 to 10 minutes. Stir in the garlic and cook 1 minute.
3. Add the carrots, crushed coriander, kosher salt and 6 cups water to the pot. Stir in the miso until it dissolves. Bring mixture to a simmer and cook, uncovered, 5 minutes. Stir in the cauliflower and cook, covered, over medium-low heat until the vegetables are very tender, about 10 minutes.
4. Remove the soup from heat. Using an immersion blender, purée until smooth. (Alternatively, you can let it cool slightly, then purée in batches in a food processor or blender.) If necessary, return the puréed soup to the heat to warm through. Stir in the lemon zest and juice. Just before serving, drizzle with oil and sprinkle with chile powder, coarse sea salt and cilantro leaves.

"Such a great soup, I've cooked it for the second time in 2 weeks. Truly amazing and a healthy option."

—Vasilis K.

"Love this! Easy, filling, simple, inexpensive, and delicious."

—**Xelle**

LEMONY PEARL BARLEY SOUP

VEGAN

time 45 minutes

yield 4 servings

High in comfort, low in fuss, this pearl barley soup answers the question of what to cook when one doesn't feel like cooking. Made with pantry staples, it beams with vibrancy. Lemon transforms the hearty soup into a dish that also feels light and restorative, while dill, used generously, reinforces the citrus flavor and brings an assertive herbaceous edge. Other herbs could step in for dill; consider parsley, cilantro or chives. Spinach is added right at the end, after the heat is turned off, which ensures that the greens maintain a little bite and stay bright. The soup will thicken over time, so if you are making it ahead or have leftovers, simply loosen it up with more stock or water when reheating.

—Hetty Lui McKinnon

Extra-virgin olive oil

1 yellow onion, finely diced

2 garlic cloves, finely chopped

2 celery stalks, thinly sliced

1 cup chopped fresh dill leaves and stalks

Fine sea salt

6 ounces pearl barley (about 1 cup)

6 cups vegetable stock, store-bought or homemade (page 224)

3 to 4 tablespoons fresh lemon juice (from 1 large lemon)

Black pepper

2 ounces (about 2 cups) baby spinach

Plain Greek yogurt, vegan coconut yogurt or crème fraîche, for serving

Lemon wedges, for serving

1. Heat a large Dutch oven or heavy pot over medium-high heat. Add 1 to 2 tablespoons oil along with the onion and cook, stirring, until softened, 2 to 3 minutes. Add the garlic, celery, half the dill and ½ teaspoon salt and stir until fragrant, 1 to 2 minutes.
2. Add the pearl barley and stock and bring to the boil. Cover, reduce heat to medium and cook, stirring occasionally, until the barley is swollen and tender, 25 to 30 minutes.
3. Turn off heat. Add the lemon juice and season with salt and pepper. Taste and make sure the seasonings are to your liking, adjusting the salt and lemon juice as needed.
4. Stir in the spinach, allowing the residual heat to wilt the leaves.
5. Ladle the soup into bowls. Top with a dollop of yogurt and the remaining dill, drizzle generously with olive oil, and serve with lemon wedges alongside.

ASARO (YAM AND PLANTAIN CURRY)

VEGAN

time 50 minutes

yield 4 to 6 servings

This recipe is an adaptation of asaro, the Yoruba word for a dish of starchy root vegetables simmered in a seasoned tomato- and chile-based sauce. Regional versions are served all year round across southern Nigeria and in other parts of West Africa. Traditionally, the dish is made with the West African yam, but you can also use white or purple taro root or unripe plantains. Here, firm green plantains are combined with white yams in a sauce rich with caramelized shallots, garlic and ginger. There is slight but welcome heat from a single red habanero dropped in whole to infuse the stew. Coconut milk and an optional spoonful of red palm oil—a floral, slightly smoky oil that is pressed from the fruit of oil palm trees—round out the flavors, and hearty greens cut the richness. Serve topped with crunchy shallots, fresh herbs and freshly squeezed lime juice.

—Yewande Komolafe

¼ cup neutral oil, such as canola or grapeseed oil

4 medium shallots, thinly sliced (about 1 cup)

Salt

4 garlic cloves, smashed

1 (2- to 3-inch) piece fresh ginger, peeled and grated (about 2 tablespoons)

2 teaspoons ground turmeric

2 tablespoons tomato paste

1 whole red habanero or Scotch bonnet chile, pierced all over with a knife

1 (14-ounce) can whole peeled tomatoes with their juices

1½ pounds white or orange yams, peeled and cut into 1½-inch pieces

2 green (unripe) plantains (about 1 pound total), cut into 1½-inch pieces

1 (13-ounce) can unsweetened coconut milk

1 tablespoon red palm oil (optional)

4 cups julienned hearty greens, such as dandelion greens, collards or Tuscan kale, tough stems removed

¼ cup basil leaves, torn

¼ cup chopped cilantro leaves and tender stems

1 lime, for squeezing

1. In a medium Dutch oven or heavy pot, heat the oil over medium heat. Add the shallots and cook, stirring frequently, until caramelized and golden brown, about 5 minutes. Using a slotted spoon, carefully remove the shallots from the oil and let drain on paper towels or a cooling rack. Season with salt and set aside.
2. Pour off all but 2 tablespoons oil from the pot. (Reserve the excess shallot oil for another use.) Add the garlic, ginger and turmeric and sauté over medium-low heat until softened and fragrant, about 2 minutes. Add the tomato paste and cook, stirring constantly, for an additional 2 minutes or until it begins to stick to the bottom of the pot.

3. Drop in the habanero and add the tomatoes with their juices, crushing the tomatoes with your hands as you go. Stir to combine the ingredients and dissolve the tomato paste, then add 3 cups water and bring to a boil over high heat.
4. Once boiling, season with salt, reduce heat to medium and add the yams. Simmer until the yams are just beginning to soften, about 10 minutes. Add the plantains and cook until both vegetables are tender but hold their shape, and the liquid is slightly reduced and thickened, 15 to 18 minutes.
5. Stir in the coconut milk and red palm oil (if using), season with more salt and let simmer for another 10 minutes. Add the greens and cook until softened, 2 to 3 minutes.
6. To serve, remove and discard the habanero. Ladle the soup into bowls, top with the caramelized shallots, a scattering of basil and cilantro, and several squeezes of lime juice.

GOCHUJANG POTATO STEW

VEGAN

time 1 hour

yield 4 servings

Plush baby potatoes braised in an aromatic gochujang broth form the heart of this satisfying, vegetable-packed stew. The spice-timid can lower the amount of gochujang, the Korean red-pepper paste, and heat seekers should feel free to add more to taste at the end. Canned white beans and dark green Tuscan kale (also called lacinato or dinosaur kale), stewed with soy sauce and honey, create a deeply savory flavor that is reminiscent of South Korean gochujang jjigae, a camping favorite starring pantry staples, and dakdori tang, a gochujang-based chicken and potato stew.

—Eric Kim

2 tablespoons unsalted butter or olive oil

1 red onion, roughly chopped

Salt and black pepper

5 large garlic cloves, roughly chopped

3 tablespoons gochujang, or to taste

3 cups vegetable broth, store-bought or homemade (page 224)

2 tablespoons soy sauce

1 teaspoon honey or dark brown sugar

1 pound baby gold or fingerling potatoes, large ones halved

1 (15-ounce) can cannellini or butter beans, rinsed

1 large bunch Tuscan kale, stems and leaves chopped (about 6 packed cups)

Cooked white rice, for serving

Sour cream, for serving (optional)

Chopped fresh flat-leaf parsley, for serving (optional)

1. In a large Dutch oven or heavy pot with a lid, melt the butter over medium-high heat, then add the onion. Season with salt and pepper. Cook, stirring occasionally, until the onion starts to soften, 2 to 3 minutes. Add the garlic and gochujang and stir until heated through and fragrant, just a few seconds.
2. Stir in the broth, soy sauce, honey or brown sugar, potatoes and beans. Season with salt and pepper. Bring to a boil over high heat, then reduce heat to medium-low to maintain a gentle boil. Cover and cook for 10 minutes, then add the kale. (It will seem like a lot at first but will wilt down considerably.) Tamp down the kale, cover, and continue to boil, stirring occasionally, until the potatoes are tender and the broth is thickened to your liking, 10 to 20 minutes. Taste the broth and add more salt, pepper and gochujang as desired.
3. Serve the stew alongside white rice and, for coolness against the heat, top with a dollop of sour cream and a sprinkle of parsley (if using).

"Simple, hearty, healthy and packs a helluva flavor punch. 10/10 a new favorite in our house!"

—Tara N.

"Love, love, love this soup. I've only ever made it with asparagus, it's so good that way I don't want to mess with perfection."

—**Salserina**

SPRING MINESTRONE WITH KALE AND PASTA

time 20 minutes

yield 4 servings

This one-pot springtime minestrone combines asparagus, peas and kale with a healthy dose of fresh ginger. The ginger is optional, but it energizes the broth. This recipe is fairly flexible overall: You can swap green vegetables according to taste and toss in any type of short pasta. The pesto and Parmesan swirled in at the end provide brightness and richness, but you could also finish the soup with tapenade, sour cream, ricotta or even a splash of your favorite hot sauce.

—Kay Chun

¼ cup extra-virgin olive oil

2 large shallots or 1 small onion, thinly sliced

2 celery stalks, thinly sliced

Salt and black pepper

2 tablespoons minced fresh ginger (optional)

2 tablespoons minced garlic

2 quarts vegetable stock, store-bought or homemade (page 224)

1 cup ditalini or other small pasta (about 5 ounces)

8 ounces asparagus, sliced into ½-inch pieces, thinly sliced zucchini or chopped broccoli (about 1½ cups)

1 cup fresh or frozen peas

5 ounces baby kale, baby spinach or torn mature spinach (about 4 cups)

Store-bought pesto and grated Parmesan, for serving

1. In a large Dutch oven or heavy pot with a lid, heat the oil over medium heat. Add shallots and celery and season with salt and pepper. Cook, stirring occasionally, until softened, about 5 minutes.
2. Add the ginger (if using) and garlic and stir until very fragrant, about 2 minutes. Add the stock and bring to a simmer.
3. Stir in the pasta and cook according to package instructions until al dente. Stir in the asparagus and peas and cook until vegetables and pasta are tender, about 3 minutes longer. Stir in the kale and season with salt and pepper.
4. Divide soup among bowls. Swirl in some pesto and top with Parmesan.

BUTTERNUT SQUASH AND GREEN CURRY SOUP

VEGAN

time about 1 hour

yield 6 to 8 servings

This creamy, vibrant soup is a Thai-inspired version of the puréed squash soup you know and love. The green curry paste, which is relatively easy to find in the international aisle of the grocery store, along with coconut milk, perfectly complements the butternut squash's sweetness. But it's the topping—a spin on miang kham, a Thai and Lao snack full of peanuts, coconut and chiles—that's the real standout.

—Samin Nosrat

For the soup

4 tablespoons refined coconut oil or other neutral oil

3 medium shallots, diced

1 (2-inch) piece fresh ginger, peeled and thinly sliced

1 lemongrass stalk, cut into 3-inch pieces

Salt

2 medium butternut squash (about 4 pounds total), peeled and cut into ¾-inch cubes

2 (13-ounce) cans unsweetened coconut milk

6 to 8 tablespoons vegetarian Thai green curry paste, or to taste (see Tip)

3 tablespoons vegan fish sauce (optional; see Tip)

3 to 4 cups water or vegetable stock, store-bought or homemade (page 224), plus more as needed

For the garnish

¾ cup raw peanuts

¾ cup unsweetened raw coconut flakes

2 tablespoons vegan fish sauce (optional; see Tip)

8 small dried red chiles, such as Japones or chiles de árbol, thinly sliced

1 tablespoon neutral oil or melted coconut oil

1 tablespoon minced lemongrass

1 teaspoon granulated sugar

10 makrut lime leaves, thinly sliced (optional)

Handful of Thai or Italian basil leaves

2 to 3 limes, quartered

Tip

For the curry paste, check the label to ensure it's vegetarian/seafood-free.

Add fish sauce if you're pescatarian or omnivorous, or use vegan fish sauce.

1. Prepare the soup: Heat oven to 300 degrees. In a large Dutch oven or heavy pot with a lid, melt the oil over medium-high heat. When the oil shimmers, add the shallots, ginger, lemongrass and a generous pinch of salt. Reduce heat to low and cook, stirring occasionally, until the shallots are tender and just starting to brown, about 18 minutes.
2. Add the squash, coconut milk, curry paste, fish sauce (if using) and 3 cups water or stock. Increase heat to high. When the liquid comes to a boil, reduce to a simmer, cover and cook the soup until squash is tender, about 25 minutes.

"This, particularly the miang kham topping, is so good that my carnivore husband shrieked, 'Why have you been holding out on me for 27 years?'"

—Anthony M.

3. While the soup cooks, prepare the garnishes: In a medium mixing bowl, toss together the peanuts, coconut flakes, fish sauce (if using), chiles, oil, lemongrass, sugar and lime leaves (if using).
4. Spread the mixture out on a baking sheet in a single layer. Bake for 18 to 20 minutes, stirring every 3 minutes after the first 10 minutes. Remove from the oven when the coconut is deep golden brown and immediately transfer to a small bowl to prevent overcooking. Stir to combine, then set aside.
5. Remove the soup from heat. Remove and discard the lemongrass. Using an immersion blender, purée the soup. Alternatively, transfer the soup in batches to a blender or food processor and carefully purée. Taste and adjust for salt and curry paste. Add water or stock to thin the soup to the desired consistency.
6. Thinly slice the basil leaves and arrange on a small plate or platter, along with the lime wedges and peanut mixture. Serve the soup hot with garnishes.

"Every good recipe contains an insight and this one's is turmeric + dill; a combination I would never have thought of and which yields a delicious and fragrant soup."

—Nina

WHITE BEAN, RICE AND DILL SOUP

VEGAN

time 45 minutes

yield 6 servings

This cozy, comforting pot of soup comes together quickly with a few pantry staples. Creamy canned navy beans and jasmine rice add body to a base of softened vegetables stained with turmeric. You may be tempted to add stock, but be assured that using water is enough here. The sum of the ingredients can stand on its own and doesn't need the added boost of stock. (If you do add stock, be mindful of the amount of salt you use.) The dill—which can be fresh or dried—and turmeric liven up the soup and offer a reminder of spring any time of year.

—Naz Deravian

¼ cup extra-virgin olive oil

6 garlic cloves, roughly chopped

2 large carrots, scrubbed and finely chopped

2 celery stalks, finely chopped

1 yellow onion, finely chopped

Kosher salt, such as Diamond Crystal, and black pepper

½ teaspoon ground turmeric

Red pepper flakes, to taste (optional)

⅓ cup white jasmine rice, rinsed

2 (15-ounce) cans navy beans or cannellini beans, rinsed

¼ cup chopped fresh dill, or 1 tablespoon dried dill

Lemon, for serving (optional)

1. In a large Dutch oven or other heavy pot with a lid, heat the oil over medium heat. Add the garlic, carrots, celery and onion; season with a good pinch of salt and cook, stirring occasionally, until the vegetables have softened, about 10 minutes.
2. Add the turmeric and some red pepper flakes (if using) and cook until fragrant, about 1 minute. Add the rice, stir and cook for 1 minute. Add the beans and dill; season everything well with salt (about 1½ tablespoons) and black pepper to taste. Stir and cook for 1 minute.
3. Add 6 cups of water, stir, partially cover, increase heat to high and bring to a boil. Cover completely, reduce heat to low and simmer, stirring occasionally, until the rice is completely soft and has released its starchy goodness, and the beans are creamy on the inside, about 30 minutes. Taste for seasoning as the soup simmers. Serve with lemon, if you like.

SOMEN NOODLE SOUP WITH MUSHROOMS

time 20 minutes

yield 2 servings

The perfect salve for cold winter days, this noodle soup can be cobbled together in an instant from the contents of a well-stocked kitchen. It takes its flavor from a quick bouillon made with just four ingredients: soy sauce, sesame oil, scallions and shiitakes, which deliver a hefty, flavorful dose of glutamate. Poached eggs add richness to the clean and comforting broth. Fresh eggs have stronger, firmer albumen (egg whites) and will hold their shape better than older eggs, which have a tendency to unfurl. The key to achieving a teardrop shape during poaching is allowing the eggs to simmer undisturbed.

—Sue Li

2 tablespoons vegetable oil

3 scallions, white and green parts separated and thinly sliced

8 ounces fresh shiitake mushrooms, stems discarded and caps thinly sliced (about 3 cups)

Salt

1 medium bok choy (about 4 ounces), cut into bite-size pieces

3 tablespoons soy sauce

2 teaspoons toasted sesame oil, plus more for serving

2 bundles somen or any thin wheat or rice noodles (about 7 ounces total)

2 large eggs

1. Bring a large saucepan of water to a simmer over medium-high heat.
2. In a medium heavy pot with a lid, heat the vegetable oil over medium heat. Add the scallion whites and sliced mushrooms, season with salt and cook until browned, stirring occasionally, 5 to 6 minutes.
3. Add 3 cups water to the pot and bring to a simmer over medium-high heat. Add the bok choy and cook until crisp-tender, about 1 minute. Stir in the soy sauce and sesame oil and season to taste with salt. Turn off heat and cover to keep warm.
4. Meanwhile, cook the noodles according to package instructions in the simmering water in the saucepan. Using a slotted spoon or spider, divide the noodles between two bowls. Reduce the heat to medium-low and keep the water at a simmer. Crack each egg into its own small bowl. Using a wooden spoon, stir the simmering water to create a vortex. Add the eggs, one right after the other, and cook undisturbed until the whites are set, but the yolks are still runny, about 3 minutes. With the slotted spoon, transfer the eggs to the noodle bowls.
5. Ladle the shiitake broth into the bowls. Top with the scallion greens, drizzle with sesame oil and serve.

"This is just sooo dang satisfying and easy."

—dori

"Under no circumstances skip the pickled onions!"

—**Filip**

COCONUT BLACK BEAN SOUP

VEGAN

time 35 minutes

yield 4 servings

Earthy black bean soup gets a plush makeover with the addition of canned coconut milk, which lends richness and a sweet, mellow flavor. Whole cumin seeds and tomato paste add depth, while jalapeño contributes both brightness and heat to the pot. You can purée the soup until it's velvety smooth, or leave it a little chunky. Either way, it makes for a satisfying and hearty weeknight meal.

—Melissa Clark

1 white onion

1 lime, halved

1¾ teaspoons Diamond Crystal kosher salt, or ¾ teaspoon coarse kosher salt, plus more to taste

1 tablespoon extra-virgin olive oil

4 garlic cloves, minced

1 jalapeño, minced (seeded, if desired)

1 bunch cilantro, stems and leaves separated

1 tablespoon tomato paste

1 teaspoon cumin seeds

½ teaspoon black pepper

3 (15-ounce) cans black beans, drained

1 (13-ounce) can full-fat unsweetened coconut milk

1 cup vegetable stock, store-bought or homemade (page 224), plus more if needed

1 lime, cut into wedges

1. Cut the white onion in half lengthwise and then cut lengthwise again into quarters. Thinly slice one-quarter of the onion. Add the slices to a small bowl and stir in the juice of half a lime and ¼ teaspoon salt. Set aside for serving. Dice the remaining onion and reserve.
2. Heat a large Dutch oven or heavy pot over medium-high heat. Once hot, add the oil. Add the diced onion and cook until tender and golden at the edges, 3 to 5 minutes. Stir in the garlic and cook for 1 minute or until fragrant.
3. Stir in the jalapeño. Mince ¼ cup cilantro stems and add to the pot. Cook until the jalapeño and cilantro stems are tender, about 2 minutes. Stir in the tomato paste, cumin seeds, black pepper and remaining 1½ teaspoons salt. Cook for 1 to 2 minutes, until the tomato paste darkens.
4. Add the black beans, coconut milk and stock. Bring to a boil, then reduce heat to a simmer. Simmer for 15 to 20 minutes, or until the mixture is thick.
5. Using an immersion blender or blender, purée the soup until half-smooth and still a little chunky. Add more stock if you want a brothier soup.
6. Stir in the juice of the remaining lime half. Chop the cilantro leaves and add ½ cup to the pot, reserving the rest for garnish. Taste and add more salt as needed. Serve with the sliced onions, cilantro and lime wedges.

BROCCOLI-QUINOA SOUP WITH TURMERIC AND GINGER

VEGAN

time 40 minutes

yield 4 servings

Turmeric and ginger are generous ingredients: You need only a little to deliver plenty of complex, comforting flavor. They work together in this recipe to bring warmth, earthiness, smokiness and spice to this hearty soup. Often a salad ingredient, quinoa proves its versatility here, providing a substantial and protein-packed foundation. The quinoa will continue to absorb the broth once the cooking is complete, so serve immediately for the ideal broth-to-quinoa ratio. (However, if you plan to prepare this soup ahead of time, you can simply thin it out with a little water or stock when reheating.) There's a lovely finishing touch: The chile oil cuts through the richness of the coconut milk and adds to the vibrant colors of this dish.

—Hetty Lui McKinnon

Extra-virgin olive oil

1 yellow onion, finely diced

1 (2-inch) piece fresh ginger, peeled and finely chopped

2 garlic cloves, finely chopped

1 cup white quinoa, rinsed

1½ teaspoons ground turmeric

Kosher salt, such as Diamond Crystal

4 to 5 cups vegetable stock, store-bought or homemade (page 224)

1 head broccoli (about 12 ounces)

1 (13-ounce) can unsweetened coconut milk

Black pepper

Handful of cilantro leaves, for serving

Chile oil, for serving

1. Heat a large Dutch oven or heavy pot with a lid over medium heat. When hot, add 1 tablespoon oil and the onion and cook until softened, 3 to 4 minutes. Add the ginger and garlic and stir until fragrant and soft, about 2 minutes. Add the quinoa, turmeric and 1 teaspoon salt; stir to coat the quinoa.
2. Stir in 4 cups stock, bring to a boil over high heat, then reduce heat to a simmer. Cover and cook until the quinoa is swollen and tender, about 15 minutes.
3. Meanwhile, cut the broccoli into small florets. If there is a stalk, remove the woody skin, then slice into disks.
4. Add the broccoli and coconut milk to the soup and stir. Simmer until the broccoli is just tender but still bright green, 4 to 5 minutes. This is a thick soup, but you can add more stock to thin it out, if desired. Season with salt and lots of pepper.
5. Ladle into bowls, top with cilantro and drizzle with chile oil. Serve immediately.

"The broccoli for added crunch and texture is genius. Bright, healthy, warming, and inexpensive!"

—Emily

"What a divine little recipe . . . This literally took me 30 minutes from opening the recipe to putting it in the bowl."

—Ms. Potato Head

BROTHY THAI CURRY WITH SILKEN TOFU AND HERBS

VEGAN

time 30 minutes

yield 6 servings

Jarred red curry paste is the central flavor in this wonderfully restorative and nourishing broth. Coconut milk lends a subtle creaminess, and the cherry tomatoes become bright little jammy bursts. You can use fresh tomatoes when in season, but canned tomatoes do just as well. Ladle the piping hot broth over seasoned tofu and fresh herbs: The delicate silken tofu used here will absorb a lot of flavor from the broth.

—Yewande Komolafe

2 (14-ounce) blocks silken tofu, drained

2 tablespoons neutral oil, such as grapeseed oil

2 shallots, minced

3 garlic cloves, sliced

1 (1-inch) piece fresh ginger, scrubbed and grated

3 tablespoons vegetarian red curry paste

1 (14-ounce) can cherry tomatoes, or 2 cups fresh cherry tomatoes

1 quart vegetable stock, store-bought or homemade (page 224)

1 (13-ounce) can full-fat unsweetened coconut milk

Salt

¼ cup soy sauce

Black pepper

1½ cups mixed fresh herbs, such as cilantro, basil and dill

2 scallions, trimmed and thinly sliced

Lime wedges, for serving

1. Pat the tofu blocks dry with a clean kitchen towel or paper towels. Cut each block into 3 slices.
2. Heat a medium Dutch oven or heavy pot over medium-high heat. Add the oil and shallots, and stir until softened, 2 minutes. Add the garlic, ginger and curry paste, stir, and cook until fragrant and the paste turns deep red, 2 minutes. Add the tomatoes, stir and bring to a simmer. Simmer until the tomato juices thicken slightly, 4 minutes.
3. Pour in the stock and stir. Increase heat to high and bring to a boil, then reduce heat to medium and simmer until the liquid is slightly reduced, 10 minutes. Stir in the coconut milk, season to taste with salt and remove from heat.
4. While the broth is simmering, break each tofu slice into 4 or 5 pieces and divide among six bowls. Season each bowl with 2 teaspoons soy sauce and a few cracks of pepper. Top with about ¼ cup mixed herbs.
5. Ladle the hot broth and tomatoes over the tofu. Top with sliced scallions and serve hot, with lime wedges alongside for squeezing.

CHAPTER 5

MEATLESS MONDAYS

At this writing, there are more than 4,000 emails in the inbox of *The Veggie*. I've read them all, so I know their most prevalent themes. There are ingredient swap questions, future newsletter suggestions and oh-so-many hyper-specific, situational recipe requests. In this book, I set out to answer many of them, dedicating whole chapters to the most frequent questions. But there is one email that stands out, succinctly titled "Request":

"Southern fried chicken with no chicken. Thanks."

If you've catered to a meat-and-potatoes type before (or, frankly, a small child), you know that an all-vegetables affair can be a tough sell. So for those new to vegetarian or vegan endeavors, recipes with familiar silhouettes are particularly appealing. Call 'em meat-shaped.

In the pages ahead, we make the ultimate swaps: Out comes chicken or beef or, in the case of the Coconut Saag (page 148), even cheese. In go meaty portobello mushrooms, tender beans and, of course, plenty of tofu.

We're not here to trick ourselves. There is, admittedly, no Southern fried chicken recipe using plant-based meats ahead. (But there are Nashville-Style Hot Tofu Sliders in the Plate Optional chapter on page 102, if that speaks to you. And it should.) We're here to revel in the chameleonic nature of vegetables and plant proteins and to realize that, with the help of the right recipe, they have more range than anything you can pick up at the butcher counter.

It's amazing what a recognizable sauce or flavor profile can do. The Kung Pao Tofu (page 144) might leave you wondering why you ever made the dish with chicken to begin with. The Eggplant Bolognese (page 158), teeming with eggplant, mushrooms, carrots, tomato and onion, achieves a richness that might surprise you. And the Chickpea Picadillo (page 141), the vegetarian cousin of a frugal and flavorful favorite from my childhood, will fill you up like the original with the help of beans, mushrooms and tofu.

But if you do need to trick others? I won't tell.

BASIL TOFU
PAGE 138

CHICKPEA PICADILLO
PAGE 141

CABBAGE PARM
PAGE 142

KUNG PAO TOFU
PAGE 144

PORTOBELLO AU POIVRE
PAGE 147

COCONUT SAAG
PAGE 148

WHITE BEANS AU VIN
PAGE 151

VEGETARIAN TAMALE PIE
PAGE 152

SWEET AND SOUR CAULIFLOWER
PAGE 154

MUSHROOM LAAB
PAGE 157

EGGPLANT BOLOGNESE
PAGE 158

BASIL TOFU

VEGAN

time 25 minutes

yield 4 servings

This vegan riff on pad krapow, the popular Thai stir-fry of ground chicken or pork with chiles, garlic and basil, is just as robustly seasoned and satiating. The traditional dish uses holy basil, but Thai or everyday sweet basil works well here. The cooking of this dish happens quickly, so have all your ingredients prepped beforehand. Tear the tofu into chunky pieces, as it will naturally break down further while being stir-fried. Keep the flavor of the basil bright and the color green by adding it right at the end, so the leaves are barely kissed with heat. Thai chiles are spicy, so add according to your taste: Two is a good choice for those who like some heat, or three if you like it fiery.

—Hetty Lui McKinnon

2 tablespoons vegetable or grapeseed oil

1 shallot or small red onion, sliced

1 red bell pepper, halved, finely diced

4 ounces green beans, trimmed and sliced into ½-inch pieces

Kosher salt, such as Diamond Crystal

4 garlic cloves, finely chopped

2 to 3 Thai green chiles, finely chopped

2 (14- to 16-ounce) packages extra-firm tofu, drained and torn into irregular 1-inch pieces

2 tablespoons soy sauce

2 tablespoons dark soy sauce

2 tablespoons lime juice

1 cup fresh Thai, holy or sweet basil leaves

Cooked jasmine or short-grain white rice, for serving

1 lime, quartered, for serving

1. Heat a wok or large skillet over medium-high. When it's hot, drizzle in the oil, then add the shallot and cook, tossing, until softened, about 1 minute. Add the bell pepper and green beans, season with ½ teaspoon salt and cook, tossing, for 1 minute. Add the garlic and Thai chiles and cook until fragrant, about 1 minute.
2. Add the tofu, soy sauce and dark soy sauce and stir-fry until the tofu is well coated and warmed through, 3 to 4 minutes. Finally, add the lime juice and basil leaves and toss until the basil is wilted, about 30 seconds.
3. Serve with rice and lime wedges.

"What a delicious and surprising combo of flavors!"

—Shazam

“Unbelievably delicious. Seriously, I could not believe how these flavors came together to create this.”

—Cece

CHICKPEA PICADILLO

VEGAN

time 40 minutes

yield 4 servings

This plant-based take on a Mexican picadillo trades the traditional ground meat for a deeply savory mix of mushrooms, tofu and chickpeas, simmered with tangy tomatillos, poblano and scallions until everything melds into a rich, comforting hash. A box grater gives the tofu a ground meat-like texture that crisps beautifully in the pan, while the tomatillos add a tart freshness that keeps each bite lively and light. This weeknight-friendly dish is flavorful and deeply satisfying—especially when served alongside rice and beans or made into tacos or burritos.

—Rick A. Martínez

6 tablespoons extra-virgin olive oil

8 ounces mushrooms, such as cremini, chopped

1 (12-ounce) block extra-firm tofu, drained and grated on the large holes of a box grater

5 large scallions, trimmed and chopped, white and green parts separated

1 medium poblano chile, seeded and chopped

1 to 2 jalapeños, chopped (use 1 seeded jalapeño for a milder dish, 2 with seeds for medium heat)

3 garlic cloves, finely chopped

6 ounces tomatillos (about 3), husked, rinsed and chopped

Salt

1½ cups vegetable stock, store-bought or homemade (page 224), or mushroom stock

1 (15-ounce) can chickpeas, with the liquid

¼ cup chopped cilantro leaves and tender stems

1. In a large well-seasoned cast-iron or nonstick skillet with a lid, heat 2 tablespoons oil over high heat. Cook mushrooms, tossing occasionally, until browned on all sides, 6 to 8 minutes. Transfer to a medium bowl.
2. In the same pan, heat 2 tablespoons oil and cook the tofu, tossing occasionally, until any liquid has evaporated and the edges are browned, 6 to 8 minutes. Transfer to the bowl with the mushrooms.
3. In the same pan, heat remaining 2 tablespoons oil and add the scallion whites, poblano, jalapeños, garlic and tomatillos. Season with salt and cook, tossing occasionally, until the scallions are just starting to brown and the tomatillos begin to break down, about 5 minutes.
4. Reduce heat to medium-high and return the mushrooms and tofu, along with any juices, to the pan. Stir in the stock and the chickpeas along with their liquid. Cook, stirring and scraping up browned bits, until all the vegetables are tender and most of the liquid has evaporated, 15 to 20 minutes. Season with more salt if needed. Mix in the cilantro and the scallion greens just before serving.

Tip

Picadillo (without cilantro or scallion greens) can be refrigerated in an airtight container for up to 2 days or frozen for up to 3 months. Reheat in the microwave or in a small saucepan, covered, on low.

CABBAGE PARM

time 50 minutes

yield 4 servings

Cabbage confirms its status as one of the vegetable kingdom's most versatile members in this untraditional yet deeply comforting dish. Roasted at high temperature, the cabbage becomes sweet and smoky, providing a complex vegetarian foundation for the classic Parmesan treatment more often applied to eggplant or mushrooms. The usual bread crumbs are replaced with chunky croutons, which deliver crunch—and it's a good idea to make extra for soaking up the sauce or even just for snacking. Experiment with different varieties of cabbage; conical Caraflex will deliver a sweeter finish, while savoy, with its looser leaf structure, has a milder flavor and can cook in less time.

—Hetty Lui McKinnon

7 tablespoons extra-virgin olive oil, plus more for serving

1 medium head green cabbage (about 2½ pounds), cut into 2-inch wedges

Salt and black pepper

½ pound loaf crusty bread, such as sourdough or ciabatta, torn into 1-inch chunks

1 garlic clove, grated

3 cups store-bought or homemade tomato sauce

8 ounces low-moisture mozzarella, grated (about 2 cups)

Basil leaves, for topping

1. Place oven racks in the middle and bottom of the oven and heat the oven to 450 degrees.
2. Drizzle a sheet pan with 2 tablespoons oil, then arrange the cabbage wedges on the pan, setting each one flat. Drizzle the top and sides of the cabbage with 3 tablespoons oil and season with salt and pepper. Place on the middle rack and roast until tender and golden, 25 to 35 minutes.
3. Place the torn bread on another sheet pan. Add the garlic, drizzle with remaining 2 tablespoons oil, season with salt and pepper and toss well to coat evenly. Place on the bottom rack and cook for 5 minutes. Remove from the oven, toss the croutons and return to the oven until golden and crispy, 8 to 10 minutes.
4. Remove the cabbage from the oven and spoon the tomato sauce over. Top with the mozzarella and return to the oven until the cheese is melted and golden, 10 to 15 minutes.
5. To serve, scatter croutons and basil leaves over the cabbage and drizzle with more oil. Serve immediately.

"This is genuinely so good. Leave all your assumptions around cabbage at the door and don't skimp on the croutons!"

—Susannah

KUNG PAO TOFU

VEGAN

time 1 hour

yield 3 to 4 servings

Fiery with dried chiles, tingly with Sichuan peppercorns and studded with peanuts, this recipe is a vegan take on the Chinese American restaurant classic, kung pao chicken. Though variations of this dish abound, this version swaps in tofu for chicken, treating the tofu similarly. Pressing the tofu removes excess moisture, leaving more room for flavor to penetrate and lending a denser, chewier texture. The cornstarch coating helps the tofu brown and crisp, acting as a sponge for the savory, spicy, tingly sauce.

—Ham El-Waylly

1 (14-ounce) block extra-firm tofu

¼ cup soy sauce

2 tablespoons brown sugar

2 tablespoons hoisin sauce

2 tablespoons sake or other rice wine

1 tablespoon black vinegar or unseasoned rice vinegar

2 teaspoons toasted sesame oil

½ teaspoon freshly ground white pepper, or ¼ teaspoon finely ground white pepper

3 garlic cloves, finely grated

1 (1-inch) piece fresh ginger, peeled and finely grated

2 teaspoons cornstarch (for the sauce) plus ¼ cup (for the tofu)

Salt

Grapeseed oil or other neutral oil, for sautéing

1 red bell pepper, cut into ½-inch squares

2 celery stalks, cut into ¼-inch slices

4 scallions, trimmed and cut into 1-inch chunks

1 teaspoon Sichuan peppercorns (optional)

4 Tianjin chiles or chiles de árbol, crushed

⅓ cup roasted peanuts

¼ cup roughly chopped cilantro leaves and tender stems

White rice, for serving

1. Drain the tofu, wrap in a clean kitchen towel, set on a plate and place a cast-iron skillet or other weighty object on top. Let it press for at least 10 minutes and up to 1 hour.
2. Meanwhile, prepare the sauce: In a medium bowl, whisk together the soy sauce, brown sugar, hoisin, rice wine, vinegar, sesame oil, white pepper, garlic, ginger, 2 teaspoons cornstarch and ⅓ cup water until combined.
3. Unwrap tofu and cut into ¾-inch cubes. Transfer to a medium bowl, season with salt and coat in ¼ cup cornstarch.
4. In a large cast-iron skillet over medium-high heat, pour in enough neutral oil to coat the bottom of the pan. When the oil starts shimmering, add the tofu. Cook until the bottom is golden brown and crisp, about 3 minutes, then flip. Cook until

the other side is crisp and golden brown, another 3 minutes. Remove with a slotted spoon and transfer to a plate.

5. Add the bell pepper, celery and scallions to the skillet. Cook, stirring occasionally, until the bell pepper starts to soften while maintaining some bite and the vegetables begin to char, about 4 minutes. Add the Sichuan peppercorns (if using) and chiles and cook until fragrant, about 1 minute. Add the tofu and sauce and stir to coat. Bring to a simmer and cook until the sauce thickens, about 2 minutes. Finish with the peanuts and cilantro, stir again, then serve immediately with rice.

"This is great! My husband likes it better than Steak au Poivre (say what?)!"

—Lisa

PORTOBELLO AU POIVRE

time 25 minutes

yield 4 servings

Steak au poivre, a classic French dish of peppercorn-crusted steak with cream sauce, seems like it was meant to be made with mushrooms. Not only do mushrooms sear well, but they're also a friend to the dish's main flavorings: heavy cream, heady spices and warming liquor. For the best results, crisp the mushrooms first in a hot pan, baste them with garlic butter until tender, then let them simmer in the cream sauce so they soak up that richness. Serve with roasted, mashed or fried potatoes, a salad of watercress or another spicy green and red wine, of course.

—Ali Slagle

4 large portobello mushrooms, stems and gills discarded

¼ cup olive oil

2 teaspoons black pepper

4 tablespoons unsalted butter, plus more as needed

3 garlic cloves, roughly chopped

Salt

1 shallot, finely chopped

¼ cup Cognac or another brandy

¾ cup heavy cream

1 tablespoon Dijon mustard

1. Brush the mushrooms all over with the oil. Sprinkle the pepper evenly over the gill sides (about ½ teaspoon per mushroom). Heat a large cast-iron skillet over medium-high heat, then add the mushrooms gill side up and sear until the underside is browned and the gill side looks wet, 3 to 6 minutes. Flip and cook until golden and the pepper is fragrant, 2 to 4 minutes.
2. Reduce heat to medium-low. Flip the mushrooms so they're gill side up, then add the butter and garlic, and season with salt. Continue to cook, tilting the skillet to baste the mushrooms with the butter and garlic, until tender, 2 to 5 minutes. Transfer the mushrooms to a plate, leaving the butter in the skillet.
3. Add the shallot to the pan and stir until softened, 2 to 4 minutes, adding a little more butter if the pan looks dry. Stand back and carefully add the Cognac—it may flame. Stir until the Cognac has nearly evaporated. Add the cream and mustard, season with salt, and stir to combine. Return the mushrooms to the pan gill side down, and cook until the cream is thickened and the color of a latte, 2 to 4 minutes. Serve the mushrooms with a drizzle of the sauce.

COCONUT SAAG

VEGAN

time 35 minutes

yield 4 servings

Saag paneer is a classic North Indian dish—but it's also endlessly riffable. Swap out the paneer for feta or halloumi, the mustard greens for kale or spinach, and so on. This is a particularly stellar riff, in which coconut milk enriches an already aromatic and verdant sauce that can be paired with extra-firm tofu (or the traditional paneer). The final hit of coconut oil infused with smoky cumin seeds and red chile powder adds loads of depth, making this dish quite possibly the most luxurious way to eat a pound of greens.

—Priya Krishna

3 tablespoons vegetable oil

2 tablespoons coriander seeds

3 green cardamom pods, or ¼ teaspoon ground cardamom (freshly ground is best)

1 yellow onion, roughly chopped

1 (½-inch) piece fresh ginger, peeled and roughly chopped

2 garlic cloves, minced

1 pound mustard greens, tough ends trimmed and greens roughly chopped, or fresh baby spinach (10 to 12 cups)

Juice of ½ lime

1 small Indian green, serrano or bird's eye chile, roughly chopped

1 teaspoon coarse kosher salt

1 (13-ounce) can unsweetened coconut milk

1 (12-ounce) block extra-firm tofu (or 1 [8-ounce] package paneer), drained and cut into ½-inch cubes

1½ tablespoons coconut oil

2 teaspoons cumin seeds

¼ teaspoon asafetida (optional, but really fantastic)

¼ teaspoon red chile powder, such as cayenne or Kashmiri

Rice or roti, for serving

1. In a large Dutch oven or heavy, deep pan over medium heat, warm the vegetable oil. Once it shimmers, add the coriander seeds and cardamom pods and toast the spices until fragrant and starting to brown, about 2 minutes. Add the onion and cook until soft and translucent, 5 to 6 minutes, stirring occasionally. Stir in the ginger and garlic and cook until fragrant, 1 minute more.
2. Add the mustard greens, a large handful at a time, and cook until just wilted and still bright green. Don't overcook the greens!
3. Remove the pan from heat and stir in the lime juice, chile and salt. Let cool for a few minutes, then transfer to a blender (or use an immersion blender) and blend to a chunky paste. Return the mixture to the pan over low heat. Stir in the coconut milk, then gently stir in tofu. Cook for 5 to 7 minutes more, until the tofu is warmed through and has soaked up some of the sauce.

"Saag paneer is one of my favorite dishes, but I've never been able to make a truly great version at home. This recipe broke that curse."

—Amanda

4. While the tofu cooks, in a small pan or butter warmer over medium-high heat, melt the coconut oil. Add the cumin seeds and, once they start to brown and dance around in the pan, about 1 minute, remove the pan from heat and stir in the asafetida (if using) and chile powder.
5. Pour the coconut oil mixture over the saag and serve with rice or roti.

"Very yummy and easy to make, and really does taste like Coq au Vin."

—Shari

WHITE BEANS AU VIN

VEGAN

time 45 minutes

yield 4 servings

This recipe uses canned white beans in place of chicken for a quick and totally meatless riff on classic coq au vin that is easily made vegan with a butter replacement. Mushrooms, red wine, Cognac and a splash of balsamic vinegar stirred in just before serving help this dish develop an impressive depth of flavor in just a short time. The quality of your vegetable broth makes a big difference here; use a good-quality brand, preferably organic, for best results.

—Lidey Heuck

3 tablespoons unsalted butter, plant-based butter or oil

3 medium carrots, cut into ½-inch dice (about 1½ cups)

5 medium shallots, chopped (about 1 cup)

Kosher salt and black pepper

8 ounces cremini mushrooms, quartered

5 thyme sprigs

3 garlic cloves, minced

½ cup dry red wine, such as Côtes du Rhône (to make vegan, look for a vegan wine)

2 teaspoons tomato paste

2 (15-ounce) cans cannellini beans, rinsed and drained

2 cups low-sodium vegetable broth, store-bought or homemade (page 224)

1 tablespoon Cognac or brandy

2 tablespoons chopped fresh parsley, plus more to taste

1 teaspoon balsamic vinegar

1. In a large Dutch oven or heavy pot with a lid, melt the butter over medium heat. Add the carrots and shallots, season to taste with salt and pepper and cook, stirring occasionally, for 5 minutes.
2. Add the mushrooms and cook, stirring occasionally, until all the vegetables are tender, 5 to 7 minutes.
3. Add the thyme sprigs and garlic, and cook until fragrant, about 30 seconds. Add the wine and tomato paste and cook, stirring occasionally, until the wine is almost completely evaporated, 2 to 3 minutes.
4. Add the beans, broth, Cognac, 1 teaspoon salt and ½ teaspoon pepper and bring to a boil over medium-high heat. Reduce heat to low, partly cover, and simmer, stirring occasionally, until the sauce has reduced and thickened, 25 to 30 minutes.
5. Remove and discard the thyme sprigs. Off the heat, stir in the parsley and vinegar. Season to taste with salt and pepper. Divide among shallow bowls, sprinkle with more parsley, if desired, and serve.

VEGETARIAN TAMALE PIE

time 1 hour

yield 6 to 8 servings

Not to be confused with Latin American tamales, tamale pie is a comforting retro casserole made from ground beef chili that is topped with cornbread batter and then baked. This vegetarian version relies on vegetables and beans instead of meat. Fresh green chiles and onions are broiled until charred to deepen their flavor, then puréed with tomatoes to make a complex sauce for the beans. The cornbread topping—crisp at the surface, tender underneath—gets an optional handful of Cheddar sprinkled on top for added verve. Serve this one-pot meal on its own or with a creamy dollop of sour cream or yogurt on the side.

—Melissa Clark

For the chili

1 red or white onion, halved

2 jalapeños, halved lengthwise (seeded, if desired)

1 poblano or green bell pepper, halved lengthwise, seeds removed

2 tablespoons extra-virgin olive oil, plus more for brushing

1¾ teaspoons kosher salt, such as Diamond Crystal, plus more as needed

1 (28-ounce) can whole or diced plum tomatoes

3 large garlic cloves, finely grated or minced

2 tablespoons mild or hot chili powder, plus more as needed

2 teaspoons dried oregano

1¾ teaspoons ground cumin

3 (15-ounce) cans black or pinto beans, drained and rinsed

1 cup chopped cilantro leaves and tender stems (optional)

For the cornbread

¾ cup/135 grams fine cornmeal

2 tablespoons all-purpose flour

1½ teaspoons baking powder

½ teaspoon kosher salt

1 large egg, at room temperature

⅓ cup/80 grams sour cream or plain whole-milk yogurt, plus more for serving

¼ cup/57 grams unsalted butter, melted and cooled

2 teaspoons honey

2 scallions, whites and greens thinly sliced, plus more for serving

1 cup grated Cheddar (optional)

1. Prepare the chili: Place a rack as close to the heating element as possible and heat the broiler. Cover a baking sheet with foil. Finely dice half of the onion and set aside for later.
2. Slice remaining onion half into ½-inch-thick half-moons and arrange on the prepared baking sheet. Place the jalapeños and poblano next to the onions, cut sides down. Lightly brush the vegetables with oil and sprinkle with a pinch of salt.

"I mention the words Tamale Pie and everyone shouts out hooray! It's delish as written but I now double the cornbread topping recipe."

—**Blair**

Broil 2 to 4 minutes, until vegetables are charred on one side. (If the peppers are small, they will be charred after 1 to 2 minutes.) Flip vegetables and broil until the other side is charred, 1 to 3 minutes.

3. Transfer the pan to a rack until cool enough to handle, then stem the peppers. Transfer the charred vegetables and any accumulated juices to a blender (or use a bowl and immersion blender). Add the tomatoes and ¼ teaspoon salt and blend to a coarse purée. Set aside. (You can make this up to 4 days ahead and store in the refrigerator until needed.)
4. Heat the oven to 425 degrees. In a large Dutch oven or heavy pot, heat the 2 tablespoons oil over medium-high heat. Add diced onion and sauté until lightly browned, 6 to 9 minutes. Add the garlic and cook until fragrant, about 1 minute. Stir in the chili powder, oregano, remaining 1½ teaspoons salt and the cumin and cook until spices darken, about 30 seconds.
5. Add beans and the reserved tomato purée and let the mixture simmer until thick and chili-like, 10 to 15 minutes. Stir in cilantro (if using). Taste and add more salt and chili powder, if needed.
6. While the chili simmers, prepare the cornbread: In a medium bowl, whisk together the cornmeal, flour, baking powder and salt.
7. In a small bowl, whisk together the egg, sour cream, butter and honey. Whisk the egg mixture into cornmeal mixture until combined. Fold in the scallions.
8. Spread the cornbread topping over the chili, then top with the grated cheese (if using). Bake until the cornbread is golden brown, 20 to 25 minutes. Serve hot or warm, topped with sour cream and more scallions.

SWEET AND SOUR CAULIFLOWER

VEGAN

time 30 minutes

yield 4 servings

Reminiscent of classic sweet and sour dishes served at Chinese American restaurants, this recipe swaps in cauliflower for pork or chicken. For beautifully burnished florets with crispy edges, the cauliflower is treated to a simple dusting of cornstarch, applied in stages to create a more even coating, and a gentle lick of oil before baking or air-frying. Punchy and tart, this sweet and sour sauce is a keeper. Ketchup is the key ingredient, and it brings sourness, sweetness and umami to a simple blend of garlic, rice vinegar, soy sauce and sugar. Eat with rice, noodles or on top of pan-fried tofu.

—Hetty Lui McKinnon

6 tablespoons cornstarch (for the cauliflower) plus 1 teaspoon (for the sauce)

1 large cauliflower (about 2 pounds), cut into bite-size florets

Salt and black pepper

Extra-virgin olive oil

3 tablespoons ketchup

3 tablespoons sugar

2 tablespoons unseasoned rice vinegar

2 tablespoons soy sauce or tamari

1 garlic clove, finely chopped

2 scallions, thinly sliced

Cooked rice or noodles, for serving

1. If using an oven, heat it to 425 degrees. If using an air fryer, heat it to 400 degrees, if preheating is recommended by the manufacturer.
2. Place 3 tablespoons cornstarch in a large bowl. Add the cauliflower, season with a big pinch of salt and pepper and toss to coat. Drizzle in 2 to 3 tablespoons oil and toss until well coated. Add another 3 tablespoons cornstarch and toss. Drizzle in another 1 to 2 tablespoons oil and toss well again, making sure there is no dry cornstarch on the cauliflower.
3. If using an oven, grease a sheet pan with a drizzle of oil. Arrange the florets in a single layer on the sheet pan and roast for 10 minutes. Remove from the oven, flip the cauliflower to encourage even cooking, and return to the oven for another 8 to 10 minutes, until it is tender and golden around the edges.
4. If using an air fryer, you may need to work in batches depending on the size of your machine. Arrange the cauliflower in a single layer on the rack and air-fry for 16 minutes, tossing halfway through for even crisping. Repeat with remaining cauliflower.
5. While the cauliflower cooks, make the sweet and sour sauce: In a small pot, heat the ketchup, sugar, vinegar, soy sauce and garlic over medium heat, stirring, until the sugar melts and the mixture starts to bubble around the edges, about

1 minute. Whisk remaining 1 teaspoon cornstarch with 2 tablespoons water, then slowly pour the cornstarch slurry into the pot, stirring constantly, until the mixture thickens, about 1 minute.

6. Transfer the cauliflower to a serving bowl and drizzle the sweet and sour sauce over the florets. Top with the scallions. Serve with rice or noodles.

"My husband (big meat eater) is still talking about this dish! It's a winner."

—Tonja E.

MUSHROOM LAAB

VEGAN

time 30 minutes

yield 4 servings

Earthy mushrooms replace meat in this take on laab. A dish popular in the northern and northeastern regions of Thailand, laab (also spelled larb) is often a lively combination of cooked minced meat, fresh herbs and a punchy dressing. In this recipe, mushrooms are roasted until golden brown and crispy around the edges and, once cooled, tossed with a mix of cilantro, mint, basil and aromatics, including sliced scallions. Lime juice and soy sauce keep the dressing tangy and savory. A subtle, nutty crunch from toasted ground rice is an essential element of the salad, so don't skip this step.

—Yewande Komolafe

2 pounds mixed mushrooms, such as button, oyster, and shiitake, quartered or torn into 2-inch pieces if large

¼ cup neutral oil, such as grapeseed or vegetable oil

Salt

2 tablespoons glutinous (sweet) rice

2 limes

1 tablespoon granulated sugar

2 tablespoons soy sauce or tamari

1 garlic clove, minced

2 bird's eye chiles, sliced, or ½ teaspoon red pepper flakes

¼ cup thinly sliced red onion

¼ cup sliced scallions

¼ cup chopped fresh cilantro leaves and tender stems

½ cup fresh mint leaves, torn

½ cup fresh Thai or sweet basil leaves, torn

Steamed rice, for serving

1. Heat oven to 425 degrees.
2. Spread the mushrooms in an even layer on a sheet pan and drizzle with the oil. Season with salt and, using your fingers, toss to coat. Roast, rotating the pan halfway through, until the mushrooms are golden brown and crisp around the edges, about 25 minutes.
3. Meanwhile, in a small skillet, toast the rice over medium heat, stirring often, until it begins to smell nutty and turn golden, about 4 minutes. Remove from heat and allow to cool slightly. Transfer to a mortar and grind with a pestle to a medium-coarse powder (or process in a spice grinder).
4. In a medium bowl, zest and juice 1 lime. Add the sugar, soy sauce, garlic and chiles. Stir to dissolve the sugar. Add the roasted mushrooms to the bowl and toss to coat. Add the onion, scallions, cilantro, mint and basil. Stir to combine, then sprinkle the toasted rice powder over.
5. Cut remaining lime into wedges. Serve the mushroom laab alongside steamed rice, with lime wedges for squeezing.

EGGPLANT BOLOGNESE

time 1 hour 15 minutes

yield 4 servings

Eggplant and mushrooms come together in place of ground beef in this hearty vegetarian pasta that delivers all the depth of a traditional Bolognese sauce. Use Italian eggplant, which is widely available and has silky, sweet flesh. Peeling the eggplant helps it brown and cook more quickly and encourages it to partially melt into the sauce as it simmers. Earthy mushroom broth fortifies the vegetable-rich sauce with deep savory flavor. Serve with a simple green salad and crusty bread.

—Kay Chun

Salt and black pepper

6 tablespoons extra-virgin olive oil

1 pound Italian eggplant, peeled and cut into ¼-inch pieces (4 cups)

6 ounces cremini or white button mushrooms, finely chopped (2 cups)

½ cup finely chopped white onion

½ cup finely chopped carrot

3 garlic cloves, minced

2 tablespoons tomato paste

3 cups mushroom broth or vegetable broth, store-bought or homemade (page 224)

1 cup canned whole tomatoes, crushed by hand

1 teaspoon dried oregano

1 fresh basil sprig, plus chopped basil for serving

1 pound rigatoni, fusilli or other short pasta

2 tablespoons unsalted butter

Freshly grated Parmesan, for serving

1. Bring a large pot of salted water to a boil over high heat.
2. In a large Dutch oven or other heavy pot, heat 2 tablespoons oil over medium-high. Add half of the eggplant, season with salt and pepper and cook, stirring occasionally, until softened and lightly golden, about 5 minutes. Transfer the eggplant to a plate. Adjust the heat to medium and repeat with 2 tablespoons oil and remaining eggplant.
3. Add remaining 2 tablespoons oil and the mushrooms to the pot. Season with salt and pepper and cook, stirring occasionally and scraping up any browned bits, until golden, about 5 minutes. Add the onion and carrot, season with salt and pepper and cook, stirring occasionally, until the onion is softened, about 3 minutes. Reduce heat to low, add the garlic and tomato paste and stir until caramelized, about 2 minutes.
4. Stir in broth, tomatoes, oregano, basil sprig and the browned eggplant and bring to a boil over medium-high heat. Cover, reduce heat to medium and cook, stirring occasionally, until the eggplant is very tender, about 15 minutes. Uncover and cook, stirring and mashing half of the eggplant, until the sauce is thickened, about 2 minutes.

5. While the sauce comes to a boil, drop the pasta into the boiling water and cook according to the package directions until al dente. Reserve 1 cup pasta water, then drain the pasta.
6. Add the pasta, butter and ½ cup pasta water to the sauce and cook, stirring vigorously, until the pasta is nicely coated and the mixture is saucy, adding more pasta water if necessary, 2 to 3 minutes. Season with salt and pepper.
7. Divide the pasta among bowls. Top with cheese and chopped basil; serve warm.

CHAPTER 6

NEW COMFORTS

Whenever I return to my apartment, I'm greeted not by a devoted pet or a Lucille Ball–spirited spouse, but by an exposed, five-tier chrome shelving unit that peeks from my slim kitchen. Pantry, I'm home! Crammed with canned and dried beans, noodles and grains, spices and vinegars, various pastes and seeds, it is the ultimate salve after a day pinballing across the most overstimulating city in America. Its comforts lie in a promise: Dinner is just a few staples and minutes away.

I once believed exciting meatless meals meant hunting down elusive and ephemeral varieties of leafy greens or squash and then toting home a $50 bag. But I've learned that a life of sustained, rewarding vegetarian cooking is not built at the farm stand. It is built in the cupboard, where flavor and heft and economy reside.

Take the Creamy, Spicy Tomato Beans and Greens on page 162. Maybe on the shelf, staples like tomato paste, jarred sun-dried tomatoes, panko bread crumbs and cannellini beans don't look like much. But with a little technique, the right attitude and a burst of something fresh—peppery arugula, the lift of lemon—it starts to look a lot like a meal you'd be happy to turn over your hard-earned money for at the hot new restaurant down the street.

These are the sort of dishes I crave, not because they're easy or accessible, but because they feature the sort of elevating flourishes—browning butter, garnishing with matchsticks of fresh ginger, scorching rice until it crisps—that guarantee deliciousness.

I hope you have a quality can opener. It'll get some good working reps in with Melissa Clark's Vegetarian Skillet Chili (page 180) and her Coconut Curry Chickpeas with Pumpkin and Lime (page 183), two NYT Cooking standard-bearers awarded five stars by our readers tens of thousands of times.

What you won't need here is patience. The recipes in this chapter come in at 45 minutes or fewer. Their reliance on ingredients like orzo, canned chickpeas and jasmine rice for body, and citrus, garlic and chile crisp for depth means you need one main fresh vegetable—some asparagus, a few tomatoes, a bundle of carrots—to make a dish you're really proud of (okay, and maybe some herbs). These are budget-friendly recipes, but frugal with flavor we are not.

CREAMY, SPICY TOMATO BEANS AND GREENS
PAGE 162

BROWN BUTTER BUCATINI WITH CHARRED CABBAGE
PAGE 165

CRISPY COCONUT RICE WITH TOFU
PAGE 166

CARROT RISOTTO WITH CHILE CRISP
PAGE 168

VEGAN CACIO E PEPE
PAGE 171

LEMONY ORZO WITH ASPARAGUS AND GARLIC BREAD CRUMBS
PAGE 172

PORCINI RAGÙ
PAGE 175

CHANA MASALA
PAGE 176

CRISPY RICE WITH DILL AND RUNNY EGGS
PAGE 179

VEGETARIAN SKILLET CHILI
PAGE 180

COCONUT CURRY CHICKPEAS WITH PUMPKIN AND LIME
PAGE 183

CHEESY CABBAGE TTEOKBOKKI
PAGE 184

CRISP GNOCCHI WITH BRUSSELS SPROUTS AND BROWN BUTTER
PAGE 187

SILKEN TOFU WITH SPICY SOY DRESSING
PAGE 188

CREAMY, SPICY TOMATO BEANS AND GREENS

time 40 minutes

yield 4 servings

This weeknight wonder is for those who delight in turning a modest can of beans into a spectacular dinner. Inspired by the flavors of red pesto, this recipe calls for simmering cannellini beans with staple ingredients like onion, garlic, red pepper flakes, tomato paste and heavy cream, as well as sun-dried tomatoes and salty Pecorino cheese, until the results taste complex and rich. Top the beans with a lemony arugula salad that is peppered with fried bread crumbs for a dish that is crunchy, chewy, crispy and creamy in every bite.

—Alexa Weibel

6 tablespoons olive oil

⅔ cup panko bread crumbs

Salt and black pepper

1 yellow onion, minced

4 garlic cloves, minced

½ teaspoon red pepper flakes

⅓ cup tomato paste

2 (15-ounce) cans cannellini beans or other creamy white beans, rinsed

1 cup heavy cream

½ cup chopped jarred sun-dried tomatoes in oil

⅔ cup finely grated Pecorino cheese or Parmesan

3 ounces baby arugula (about 4 packed cups)

2 teaspoons finely grated lemon zest plus 4 teaspoons juice (from 1 lemon)

Toasted bread, for serving (optional)

1. Line a plate with paper towels. In a medium skillet, heat 2 tablespoons oil over medium heat. Stir in the panko, season with salt and pepper and cook, stirring frequently and shaking the pan, until toasted and golden, about 3 minutes. Transfer the panko to the prepared plate, then wipe out the skillet.
2. In the same skillet, heat another 2 tablespoons oil over medium heat. Add the onion, garlic and red pepper flakes, season with salt and pepper and cook, stirring frequently, until softened, about 4 minutes.
3. Add the tomato paste and stir until darkened and the mixture is combined, about 3 minutes.
4. Stir in the beans, heavy cream, sun-dried tomatoes and ⅓ cup water and simmer, stirring occasionally, until the flavors meld, about 5 minutes. Stir in ⅓ cup cheese, then season to taste with salt and pepper.
5. In a medium bowl, toss the arugula with the panko, lemon zest and juice, remaining ⅓ cup cheese and remaining 2 tablespoons oil. Season with salt and pepper. Pile the greens at the center of the bean mixture. Serve with toasted bread, if desired.

"Restaurant quality delicious! This would be the star of a dinner party or weeknight hero! 11/10!"

—KWB

"Changed my entire worldview on cabbage."
—Joe

BROWN BUTTER BUCATINI WITH CHARRED CABBAGE

time 45 minutes

yield 4 servings

Charred cabbage brings a complex mix of flavors—from savory to bitter to sweet—to this simple yet satisfying weeknight pasta. As it cooks, the cabbage turns silky, clinging to the bucatini like the most delicious of frills. The pecans play off the nutty notes of the charred cabbage and brown butter. Like cacio e pepe and other pastas that fuse melted cheese with pasta water, this dish tightens up quickly, so make sure to have plenty of pasta water on hand to loosen it as needed.

—Ham El-Waylly

Salt

2 tablespoons grapeseed oil or other neutral oil

1 small green cabbage (about 1½ pounds), halved and thinly sliced

Black pepper

12 ounces bucatini pasta

½ cup unsalted butter, cut into chunks

½ cup roughly chopped raw pecans

6 ounces coarsely grated Parmesan (about 2 cups)

⅓ cup roughly chopped fresh parsley leaves

1. Bring a large pot of water to a boil. Season with salt until it tastes like a slightly salty soup.
2. In a large skillet, heat the oil over medium-high heat until it shimmers. Add the cabbage and a large pinch of salt. Cook, stirring frequently, until the cabbage softens, shrinks and becomes deeply charred in spots, 20 to 25 minutes. Season aggressively with pepper, then taste for salt and season accordingly. Transfer the cabbage to a plate. Wipe out the skillet.
3. Add the pasta to the boiling water and cook for 1 minute less than the package instructs. Reserve 2 cups pasta water, then drain the pasta.
4. Place the butter, pecans and a pinch of salt in the same large skillet and cook over medium heat, stirring constantly, until the butter turns golden brown and smells nutty, 2 to 3 minutes. Add 1 cup pasta water, the cabbage and the cooked pasta and stir to coat. Simmer until the sauce thickens, 3 to 5 minutes. Add 1 cup Parmesan and all the parsley and stir vigorously until the sauce coats the pasta and the cheese melts. If the pasta seems too dry, add a splash of pasta water.
5. Divide among bowls and top with the remaining cheese and more pepper. Serve immediately.

CRISPY COCONUT RICE WITH TOFU

VEGAN

time 30 minutes

yield 4 servings

In many cultures, the crispy rice found at the bottom of the pot—known as concón in the Dominican Republic, tahdig in Iran and nurungji in Korea, to name just a few—is the most prized mouthful. Inspired by the simple joys of scorched rice, this easy pantry-friendly recipe calls for seasoning a mixture of cooked rice, tofu and coconut with punchy store-bought Thai curry paste, then pan-frying it until a crispy layer forms. The coconut is a surprising addition, delivering a lingering aroma that surprises in each bite. Commercial curry pastes vary in saltiness and spice, so taste yours and add accordingly, starting with 3 tablespoons and adding more if you need. The fresh elements are essential to this dish: lettuce, herbs and citrus bring welcome contrast in texture and temperature. Cold leftover rice works great in this dish.

—Hetty Lui McKinnon

4 heaping cups cold cooked white rice

3 to 4 tablespoons vegetarian red or green Thai curry paste

2 tablespoons soy sauce or tamari

1 (14-ounce) block extra-firm tofu, drained and crumbled

¾ cup shredded unsweetened coconut

1 tablespoon toasted sesame oil

4 scallions, trimmed and thinly sliced

4 makrut lime leaves, finely sliced (optional)

Salt

Neutral oil, such as vegetable or grapeseed oil

5 ounces lettuce leaves, such as romaine or butterhead

1 lemon or lime, cut into 4 wedges

Handful of mint or cilantro leaves, or both

1 long red chile, finely sliced

1. In a large bowl, mix together the rice, 3 tablespoons curry paste, soy sauce, tofu, coconut, sesame oil, scallions and makrut lime leaves (if using). Once combined, taste and add more curry paste or a pinch or two of salt, to your liking.
2. Heat a large well-seasoned cast-iron or nonstick skillet on medium-high for about 2 minutes. Add 2 tablespoons neutral oil, then add half of the rice mixture, pressing down firmly with a spatula. Let cook for 4 to 5 minutes, until a crispy golden crust has formed on the bottom. Drizzle the rice with a little neutral oil. Using a spatula, break the rice into large pieces and flip over; cook the other side for 3 to 5 minutes, until crispy. When ready, remove the first batch of crispy rice from the pan and repeat with remaining rice.
3. To serve, divide the rice among bowls and serve with lettuce, lemon, herbs and chile on the side.

"Great for a weeknight no fuss dinner, but it's so full of flavor."

—Ks

CARROT RISOTTO WITH CHILE CRISP

time 30 minutes

yield 4 servings

Simple yet surprising, this risotto is a study in contrasts: Luscious, creamy risotto is topped with caramelized carrots that are roasted with spicy chile crisp while you make the rice. The risotto base—a classic approach using shallots, garlic and white wine—is the foundation for a cheap though lush meal that can be cobbled together with pantry ingredients. Here, the risotto is subtly sweetened with freshly grated carrots, then topped with a pile of smoky roasted carrots. Don't underestimate the versatility of chile crisp: This tingly, crunchy condiment can animate any number of rich dishes like risotto, pizza and macaroni and cheese with a robust dose of heat. In recipes, as in life, opposites attract.

—Alexa Weibel

2¼ pounds carrots

2 tablespoons chile crisp, store-bought or homemade, plus more for serving

Kosher salt and black pepper

5 cups vegetable stock, store-bought or homemade (page 224)

4 tablespoons unsalted butter

1 shallot, minced

3 garlic cloves, finely chopped

½ teaspoon ground coriander

½ cup dry white wine

1½ cups arborio rice

2½ ounces Parmesan, finely grated (about 1¼ packed cups), plus more for serving

1. Heat the oven to 400 degrees.
2. Prep the carrots: If using food processor, roughly chop one-third of the carrots, then pulse them until they form very small confetti-like flecks no larger than ¼-inch big (you should have about 2 cups). Set aside. (You can also coarsely grate one-third of the carrots using a box grater.) Slice the remaining 1½ pounds carrots on a sharp diagonal about ¼-inch thick. Transfer to a baking sheet, then toss with the chile crisp. (If your chile crisp is predominantly crunchy bits, you can thin it with a little canola or vegetable oil, if needed.) Season the sliced carrots generously with salt and pepper and bake until tender, about 15 minutes, stirring halfway through.
3. Add the stock to a medium saucepan with a lid. Cover and warm over low heat.
4. In a separate medium saucepan, melt 2 tablespoons butter over medium-high heat. Add the reserved grated carrots, shallot, garlic and coriander and season generously with salt and pepper. Cook, stirring frequently, until very fragrant, 2 minutes.
5. Add the wine to the carrot mixture and cook, stirring occasionally, until mostly evaporated, about 3 minutes.

> “Adding this to my ‘meals to impress a date with’ list.”
>
> **—Anna**

6. Stir the rice into the carrot mixture, reduce heat to medium and cook, stirring, 2 minutes. Add 1 cup warmed stock and cook, stirring frequently, until the liquid is almost absorbed, about 3 minutes. Repeat four more times, adding warm liquid and stirring until absorbed.
7. Once the rice is tender and creamy and all the stock has been absorbed, add the cheese and remaining 2 tablespoons butter and stir vigorously until the risotto feels silky, creamy, luxurious. Season to taste with salt and pepper.
8. Divide the risotto among shallow bowls or plates and top with the roasted carrots. Serve with additional chile crisp, for drizzling on top.

"My partner is vegan and I'm not, and BOTH of us love this recipe!"

—Rachel

VEGAN CACIO E PEPE

VEGAN

time 30 minutes

yield 4 servings

This speedy vegan take on cacio e pepe utilizes a classic technique: Cook the pasta just short of al dente, reserve some of the starchy pasta water to add body to the sauce, then simmer the pasta in its sauce with a splash of pasta water, stirring vigorously until the sauce is emulsified. While many dairy-free pasta recipes look to puréed soaked cashews for their creaminess, this one cuts corners by using store-bought cashew butter. A spoonful of miso adds depth, and tangy nutritional yeast adds umami. Toasting the peppercorns boosts their flavor and softens them.

—Alexa Weibel

Salt

⅓ cup nutritional yeast

¼ cup cashew butter

2 tablespoons white miso paste

1 tablespoon whole black peppercorns

16 ounces spaghetti

¼ cup extra-virgin olive oil, plus more for drizzling

½ lemon, for finishing (optional)

1. Bring a large pot of lightly salted water to a boil over high heat. (Go easy on the salt here, since the miso added in Step 4 is high in salt.) In a small bowl, combine the nutritional yeast, cashew butter and miso and stir into a thick paste. Crush the peppercorns using the flat side of a knife. (Alternatively, you can roughly chop them or use a pepper grinder set to a coarse setting.)
2. Add the pasta to the boiling water, reduce heat to medium, and cook, stirring occasionally, until about 2 minutes shy of al dente according to package instructions. Reserve 2½ cups pasta water, then drain the pasta.
3. Pour the oil into the empty pot and heat over medium heat. Add about two-thirds of the crushed peppercorns and toast, stirring frequently, until fragrant, 2 to 3 minutes.
4. Add the miso mixture and stir, then whisk in 1¾ cups reserved pasta water until the sauce is smooth. Add the pasta to the sauce and cook over medium-high heat, tossing constantly and vigorously with tongs, until the sauce is glossy and the pasta is fully al dente, 1 to 2 minutes. Add an extra splash of reserved pasta water to keep the sauce glossy, if needed.
5. Divide the pasta among bowls. Drizzle with oil, sprinkle with remaining crushed peppercorns and squeeze the lemon over top (if using). Serve immediately.

LEMONY ORZO WITH ASPARAGUS AND GARLIC BREAD CRUMBS

time 20 minutes

yield 4 servings

Every spoonful of this pasta has a happy jumble of lemony orzo, grassy asparagus, garlicky bread crumbs, fresh herbs and salty Parmesan. The pasta and thinly sliced asparagus cook together in the same pot, then rest in a lemony dressing while the garlic bread crumbs are toasted, so the pasta has time to absorb as much flavor as possible.

—Ali Slagle

Salt

1 cup orzo

1 pound asparagus, thinly sliced on a diagonal (about ¼-inch thick)

5 tablespoons extra-virgin olive oil

1 teaspoon lemon zest plus 3 tablespoons fresh lemon juice, plus more as needed (from about 1 large lemon)

Black pepper

½ cup panko or homemade bread crumbs

1 small garlic clove, finely grated

¼ cup finely grated Parmesan, plus more for serving

½ cup fresh dill, mint or parsley leaves (or any combination), torn if large

1. Bring a medium pot of salted water to a boil. Add the orzo and cook according to package instructions until al dente. Two minutes before the orzo is done, add the asparagus. Drain the orzo and asparagus. Wipe out and reserve the pot.
2. Meanwhile, in a large bowl, stir together 3 tablespoons oil and the lemon zest and juice. Season to taste with salt and pepper. Add the drained orzo and asparagus and toss to coat. Set aside while you toast the bread crumbs.
3. In the reserved pot, heat remaining 2 tablespoons oil over medium heat. Add the panko and cook, stirring, until golden brown, 3 to 5 minutes. Remove from heat, then stir in the garlic and season with salt and pepper.
4. Stir the Parmesan and herbs into the orzo, taste, then season with salt, pepper and additional lemon juice, if desired. Top with the toasted bread crumbs and more Parmesan. Serve warm or at room temperature.

"This has become my recipe of the summer and has been served to all comers to equal acclaim!"

—**Penny**

"I keep those dried porcini in my pantry so this can be my emergency meal."

—Michael

PORCINI RAGÙ

time 45 minutes

yield 2 to 4 servings

Ixta Belfrage's porcini ragù, adapted here from her cookbook *Mezcla,* almost defies the name, because it doesn't demand hours on the stove and attains a velvety intensity in practically no time at all. Leave the dried porcini to soak and swell back to life; chop; gently fry with tomato paste, garlic, chile and parsley; rain down black pepper; swirl the pasta water and porcini broth; melt in some Parmesan and let it bubble. A dab of cream, then a slicking and coating of the pasta, and dinner is on the table.

—Ligaya Mishan

1½ ounces dried porcini mushrooms

Boiling water, for soaking

Fine sea salt

¼ cup olive oil, plus more for serving

3 garlic cloves, very finely chopped

½ teaspoon red pepper flakes, or to taste

½ cup finely chopped fresh parsley leaves and stems, plus more for serving

1½ tablespoons tomato paste

1 to 1½ teaspoons freshly ground black pepper

9 ounces dried tagliatelle nests

1½ ounces Parmesan, very finely grated (about ¾ loosely packed cup), plus more for serving

3 tablespoons heavy cream

1. In a medium bowl, cover the mushrooms with boiling water and let soak for 10 minutes. Reserve 5 tablespoons soaking liquid, then drain the mushrooms. Very finely chop the mushrooms, aiming to mimic the consistency of ground meat, then set aside. Bring a medium pot of salted water to a boil over high heat.
2. Meanwhile, place the oil, garlic, red pepper flakes, parsley and a heaping ¼ teaspoon salt into a large cold sauté pan. Set over medium-low heat and gently fry for 5 minutes until soft and lightly golden. Reduce heat if the garlic starts to brown.
3. Increase heat to medium-high, then add the mushrooms, tomato paste and black pepper (about 50 twists). Stir-fry for 3 minutes, then set aside.
4. Cook the pasta according to the package instructions until al dente. Reserve 1¾ cups pasta water, then drain the pasta.
5. Return the sauté pan with the mushroom mixture to medium-high heat, then stir in 1½ cups reserved pasta water plus the reserved porcini soaking liquid. Bring to a simmer, then let it bubble away for 3 minutes.
6. Add half the Parmesan, stirring until melted before adding the rest. Reduce heat to medium, then stir in the cream, followed by the tagliatelle. Toss over the heat until the the sauce has emulsified, 1 to 2 minutes, adding a splash more pasta water if the pasta looks dry.
7. Remove from heat and serve, finished with oil, Parmesan and sprinkling of parsley.

CHANA MASALA

VEGAN

time 40 minutes

yield 4 servings

Variations on chana masala, or spiced chickpeas, are found across South Asia. This version, particularly common in Punjab, calls for a simple spiced onion and tomato mixture, which serves as the foundation. The nutty and buttery legume benefits from a combination of dried chile powder and fresh chiles, as well as coriander and the spice blend garam masala. Thinly sliced ginger and cilantro, added upon serving, add freshness. Both canned and dried chickpeas work for this dish; in the case of the former, the resulting bowl of comfort feels nothing short of a miracle in under an hour.

—Zainab Shah

2 tablespoons ghee or neutral oil

1 tablespoon garlic paste or freshly grated garlic

1 tablespoon ginger paste or freshly grated peeled ginger

1 red onion, finely chopped

2 Thai green or bird's eye chiles, chopped

1 teaspoon cumin seeds

¼ teaspoon ground turmeric

½ teaspoon ground coriander

1 teaspoon Kashmiri or other hot red chile powder

4 ripe Roma tomatoes, finely chopped

¾ teaspoon fine sea salt

2 (15-ounce) cans chickpeas, drained, or 3 cups cooked chickpeas (see Tip)

2 cups vegetable stock, store-bought or homemade (page 224), or water

¾ teaspoon garam masala

2 tablespoons chopped cilantro leaves and tender stems

Fresh ginger, peeled and sliced into matchsticks, for serving

Rice or roti and lemon wedges, for serving (optional)

1. In a medium pot, melt the ghee over medium heat. Stir in the garlic, ginger paste and onion and cook, stirring occasionally, until the onion softens, 5 to 7 minutes. Stir in the chiles, cumin, turmeric, coriander and chile powder. Continue stirring for 30 seconds so the spices don't burn. Add the tomatoes with their juices and the salt. Increase heat to high and cook, stirring often, until the mixture is jammy, 5 to 7 minutes.
2. Stir in the chickpeas and stock. Bring to a boil, then reduce heat and simmer until the mixture has thickened slightly, 5 to 7 minutes. With the back of a spoon, smash some of the chickpeas against the inside of the pot to thicken the mixture. Continue smashing until it reaches the desired thickness.
3. To serve, sprinkle with garam masala and top with the cilantro and some ginger matchsticks. If desired, serve rice or roti and lemon wedges alongside.

Tip

If using dried chickpeas, place 1 pound in a medium bowl and cover with 3 inches of water. Stir in ½ teaspoon baking soda and soak for at least 7 hours or overnight. Drain and transfer the chickpeas to a medium pot. Cover with several inches of fresh water and simmer until tender, 1½ to 2 hours, then drain. Freeze any extra chickpeas in an airtight container for up to 6 months.

"Very homey and soothing and it was easy to throw together as a one-pot meal."

—**Paulis**

"Truly delicious and a great way to simplify one of my childhood fav dishes for small kitchen/small budget/ vegetarian dish."

—Emma

CRISPY RICE WITH DILL AND RUNNY EGGS

time 40 minutes

yield 4 servings

This one-skillet meal has crisp and herbaceous rice, creamy lima beans and pockets of jammy egg yolk. Its inspiration comes from baghali polo, a traditional Persian rice dish in which fava beans steam with rice, dill and spices (and the bottom is sometimes crisped tahdig-style). In this complete one-pan meal, the rice and lima beans are steamed and crisped in a skillet, then eggs are nestled right into the rice to cook. Lima beans are buttery like fava beans, though you could use another bean or even a vegetable (see Tip). A punchy topping, like feta or lemon, rounds out the meal.

—Ali Slagle

1 cup basmati or jasmine rice (no need to rinse)

1½ cups frozen lima beans (see Tip)

½ cup finely chopped fresh dill, or 1½ tablespoons dried dill

Kosher salt, such as Diamond Crystal, and black pepper

¼ cup extra-virgin olive oil, plus more as needed

4 large eggs

Crushed pitted green olives, sliced pickled pepperoncini, crumbled feta and/or lemon wedges, for serving

1. In a large nonstick skillet, stir together 1¾ cups water, the rice, lima beans, half the dill, 1 teaspoon salt and a few grinds of pepper. Bring to a boil over high heat, then cover tightly with a lid, sheet pan or foil, reduce heat to low and cook until rice is tender, about 17 minutes.
2. Uncover and fluff with a fork. (If using a lima bean alternative, stir it into the rice now.) Spread the rice in an even layer, then make four divots. (You'll add your eggs to them in Step 3.) Now crisp the rice: Pour the oil down the sides of the pan and into the divots, increase heat to medium and cook until the rice is golden brown at the edges, 2 to 5 minutes. If you don't see oil bubbling at the edges, drizzle in a little more.
3. Crack the eggs into the divots, cover the pan and cook until the whites are set but the yolks are still runny, 2 to 4 minutes. Season the eggs with salt and pepper. Sprinkle with remaining dill and some olives, pepperoncini, feta and/or a squeeze of lemon, as desired.

Tip

Instead of frozen lima beans, use the same amount of frozen, shelled edamame; drained cooked beans (homemade or a 15-ounce can); or chopped vegetables that cook in about 5 minutes, like spinach, green beans or celery. For any of these options, stir them into the rice at the start of Step 2.

VEGETARIAN SKILLET CHILI

VEGAN

time 30 minutes

yield 4 servings

If you keep canned beans, tomatoes, onion and garlic in your pantry, you can make this dish on any weeknight without having to shop. The pickled onions aren't strictly necessary, but they are simple to make and add a welcome tangy contrast to the beans. Pickled peppers are a fine substitute. If you have a bell pepper or jalapeño or two, chop them up and sauté them with the onions. And if you want to be fancy, grate the zest of the lime before juicing for the pickles, and stir it into the sour cream, if using.

—Melissa Clark

For the pickled onions

Juice of 1 lime

1 red onion or shallot, thinly sliced

Large pinch of kosher salt

Small pinch of granulated sugar

For the chili

Olive oil or grapeseed oil

1 onion, chopped

3 garlic cloves, or to taste, minced

1 teaspoon chile powder, plus more to taste

1 teaspoon dried oregano, plus more to taste

2 (15-ounce) cans beans, any type, drained

1 (14-ounce) can diced tomatoes with their juices

Salt

Fresh cilantro, diced avocado, lime wedges and sour cream, for garnish (optional)

1. Prepare the pickled onions: In a small bowl, combine the lime juice, onion, salt and sugar. Let sit while you make the chili.
2. Prepare the chili: Heat a large skillet over medium-high heat. Add the oil. When hot, add the onion and sauté until softened, 5 to 7 minutes. Add the garlic, chile powder and oregano and sauté until fragrant, 1 to 2 minutes longer. Add the beans and tomatoes and a few pinches of salt, then let simmer until the tomatoes break down, about 20 minutes.
3. Taste and add more salt, chile powder and oregano to taste. Serve with the pickled onions and any of the garnishes you like.

"This is easy, satisfying and very forgiving with additions of whatever is available in the fridge and pantry."

—**StilettosintheKitchen**

"This recipe is fantastic. So wonderfully flavorful and who knew? The three canned ingredients felt like a true gift!"

—Vijomo

COCONUT CURRY CHICKPEAS WITH PUMPKIN AND LIME

VEGAN

time 30 minutes

yield 4 to 6 servings

Canned pumpkin purée and coconut milk, heavily seasoned with curry spices and lots of fresh lime juice, make a sweet-sharp sauce for chickpeas. This is a rich, creamy curry that you can eat on its own or serve over rice or couscous. If you want to incorporate more vegetables, stir in some spinach, baby kale or sliced green beans during the last few minutes of cooking, letting them soften in the sauce.

—Melissa Clark

3 tablespoons neutral oil, such as sunflower or canola oil

1 onion, chopped

2 jalapeños, thinly sliced (seeded, if desired)

1 bay leaf

1 (1-inch) piece fresh ginger, peeled and minced

4 garlic cloves, minced

1½ teaspoons garam masala

1 teaspoon ground cumin

½ teaspoon ground turmeric

2 (15-ounce) cans chickpeas, rinsed

1 (13-ounce) can unsweetened full-fat coconut milk

1 (15-ounce) can pumpkin purée

Fine sea salt

¾ cup chopped fresh cilantro, plus more for serving

2 to 3 tablespoons fresh lime juice (from 1 to 2 limes)

Cooked rice or couscous, for serving (optional)

Lime wedges, for serving

1. In a large skillet, heat the oil over medium-high heat. Stir in the onion, jalapeños and bay leaf. Cook, stirring occasionally, until the onion is golden at the edges, about 8 minutes.
2. Add the ginger and garlic and cook until fragrant, about 2 minutes, stirring frequently. Stir in the garam masala, cumin and turmeric and cook for an additional 30 seconds.
3. Stir in the chickpeas, coconut milk, pumpkin, ½ cup water and 1½ teaspoons salt. Bring to a simmer and cook for 10 minutes, stirring occasionally, to let the flavors meld. (Add more water if it starts to look too thick.) Stir in the cilantro and lime juice to taste. Taste and add more salt if necessary.
4. Serve over rice (if using), with more cilantro sprinkled on top and lime wedges on the side.

CHEESY CABBAGE TTEOKBOKKI

time 30 minutes

yield 4 servings

A dish of royalty, tteokbokki consists of chewy Korean rice cakes (tteok) that are stir-fried (bokki) and slicked in a savory-sweet sauce. Sometimes the sauce is soy-sauce-based but more commonly today, as it is here, the sauce is gloriously red, spicy and gochujang-based. Traditional versions might include fish cakes and whole hard-boiled eggs, but this one leans into a base of butter-fried shallots and a layer of melted cheese covered in a crunchy blanket of raw cabbage. A parade of halved, molten-centered soft-boiled eggs bedecks the top.

—Eric Kim

3 large eggs

1 tablespoon granulated sugar

3 tablespoons gochujang

1 tablespoon soy sauce

1 large garlic clove, finely grated

3 tablespoons unsalted butter

2 large shallots, thinly sliced into rings

Salt

1 pound fresh or frozen tteok (rice cakes)

½ cup shredded cheese, such as sharp Cheddar or low-moisture mozzarella

5 ounces green cabbage, shredded (about 2 cups)

1. Bring a small pot of water to a boil over high heat. Carefully add the eggs, then reduce heat to gently simmer the eggs until soft-boiled, 7 minutes. Drain the eggs, then gently shake the pot to crack their shells. Cover the cracked eggs with cold water, then let cool enough to handle. Once cooled, peel the eggs directly in the water (they should peel easily). Drain and set aside.
2. In a small bowl, stir together the sugar, gochujang, soy sauce and garlic. Set aside.
3. In a large saucepan with a lid, melt the butter over medium-high heat. Add the shallots, season generously with salt and cook, stirring constantly, until the edges of the shallots are really brown, 5 to 7 minutes. Stir in the gochujang mixture and cook, stirring for a few seconds, just until the sauce loses its raw edge.
4. Stir in 1 cup cold water and add the tteok, making sure to separate them if stuck together. Bring to a simmer over medium-high and cook until the sauce thickens and the tteok are heated through but still chewy, 4 to 6 minutes. (Add a minute or two if using frozen rice cakes.)
5. Scatter the cheese over the sauce, followed by the cabbage—a nice, crunchy blanket of it. Cover to let the cheese melt; the cabbage will steam slightly. Halve the soft-boiled eggs and arrange them over the crunchy, cheesy cabbage. Serve directly from the pan.

"This is like Korean mac and cheese but better for you and with more flavor."

—**Molly**

"Great recipe. I normally roast my brussels sprouts in the oven but this skillet method worked great!"

—**Schaasyd**

CRISP GNOCCHI WITH BRUSSELS SPROUTS AND BROWN BUTTER

time 20 minutes

yield 4 servings

For a fantastic meal that can be ready in 20 minutes, toss together seared gnocchi and sautéed brussels sprouts with lemon zest, red pepper flakes and brown butter. The key to this recipe is in how you cook the store-bought gnocchi. No need to boil—just sear them until crisp and golden outside but still chewy inside. The resulting texture is reminiscent of fried dough. Shelf-stable and refrigerated gnocchi will both work here, but the shelf-stable ones do crisp up a bit better.

—Ali Slagle

1 pound brussels sprouts or other cruciferous vegetables, such as broccoli, cauliflower or even cabbage

1 lemon

4 tablespoons extra-virgin olive oil

Kosher salt, such as Diamond Crystal, and black pepper

½ teaspoon red pepper flakes

1 (18-ounce) package shelf-stable or refrigerated potato gnocchi

6 tablespoons unsalted butter, sliced into 6 pieces

½ teaspoon honey

Freshly grated Parmesan, for serving

1. Trim and halve the brussels sprouts.
2. Using a vegetable peeler, remove thick strips of lemon zest, then roughly chop. (You should have about 2 teaspoons chopped zest.)
3. In a large skillet with a lid, heat 3 tablespoons oil over medium-high heat. Add the brussels sprouts, season with ½ teaspoon salt and a few grinds of pepper, then arrange the brussels sprouts in an even layer, cut side down. Scatter the lemon zest over the top and cook, undisturbed, until the brussels sprouts are well browned underneath, 3 to 5 minutes. Add the red pepper flakes, stir and cook until the brussels sprouts are crisp-tender, 2 to 3 minutes. Transfer to a medium bowl.
4. In the same skillet, heat remaining 1 tablespoon oil over medium-high heat. Break up any gnocchi that are stuck together, add them to the pan and cook, covered and undisturbed, until golden brown underneath, 2 to 4 minutes. Add the butter and honey, season with salt and a generous amount of black pepper and cook, stirring, until the butter is golden, nutty-smelling and foaming, 1 to 2 minutes. Stir in the brussels sprouts until warmed through. Serve with grated Parmesan.

SILKEN TOFU WITH SPICY SOY DRESSING

VEGAN

time 5 minutes

yield 4 servings

This recipe is inspired by the many cold silken tofu dishes from East Asia, like Japanese hiyayakko and Chinese liangban tofu. This no-cook dish is a handy one to have up your sleeve, especially for warm evenings when the desire to cook is nonexistent. Silky soft tofu is draped in a punchy soy dressing, creating a lively dish with little effort. The tofu is ideally served cold, but 10 minutes at room temperature can take the edge off. Make it your own with other fresh herbs such as Thai basil, mint or shiso leaves, or add crunch with fried shallots or roasted peanuts. A salty, fermented element like vegetarian kimchi, pickled radish or ja choi, also known as zha cai, a Sichuan pickled mustard stem, would work well, too. One block of silken tofu is usually enough to feed two people, but for a more substantial meal, serve it with hot rice or noodles to create a pleasing contrast of temperatures.

—Hetty Lui McKinnon

For the spicy soy dressing

¼ cup soy sauce

1 tablespoon unseasoned rice vinegar

1 tablespoon sesame oil

1 tablespoon chile oil

1 tablespoon toasted white sesame seeds

2 teaspoons granulated sugar

1 scallion, thinly sliced

For the tofu

2 (14-ounce) blocks silken tofu, cold but not directly from the fridge

1 scallion, thinly sliced

Handful of cilantro leaves

1. Make the dressing: Combine the soy sauce, rice vinegar, sesame oil, chile oil, sesame seeds, sugar and scallion in a small bowl. Whisk until the sugar has dissolved.
2. Make the tofu: Drain the liquid from the packages of tofu, and gently tip the blocks onto a clean kitchen towel. (Try to keep the blocks in one piece, but don't worry if they fall apart—it will still taste great.) Pat with another clean kitchen towel, removing as much liquid as possible. Transfer the blocks to one large plate or two smaller plates—leave whole or cut into 1-inch cubes—and spoon the soy dressing over the top until the tofu is completely covered. Top with the scallion and cilantro and eat on its own or with rice or noodles on the side.

"Single-handedly converted me to silken tofu . . . DELICIOUS, satisfying, and so so easy to make, this recipe is a slam dunk."

—KRP

CHAPTER 7

RSVP-WORTHY

All I ever want to do, really, is party. Nothing animates me like a room full of my people hunched over a table of food so enticing that "rubbing shoulders" sheds its figurative meaning for its literal one. It's a hereditary condition. When I was growing up, my parents were the designated hosts of our street, if not the neighborhood. For New Year's, they'd roll out the red tablecloths for their guests, lining up dish after dish in a dazzling buffet.

There was not one centerpiece, but several, and they were always of the meat and seafood variety. But the dish I can call to mind and mouth just by closing my eyes, and the one I recall people asking the most for the recipe, was a side of scalloped potatoes. Through the glass baking dish, you could see the rendered fat from its ample cheeses ripple up along the edges, just like that one neighbor's aboveground backyard jacuzzi. (Do I sound jealous? I was.)

Some supporting dishes just steal the show like that. But a party menu that pledges itself to vegetables needn't be a cornucopia of sides. I often hear from readers who struggle during the holidays to find a statement vegetarian dish that can rally friends and family of all dietary proclivities around it like a Seussian roast. This chapter is for them—and their very lucky guests.

I'd be jazzed to score an invite to a party built around any one of these dishes. I myself anchored a Friendsgiving around the luxurious Creamed Greens Potpie (page 198) to ensure that a vegetarian guest felt taken care of. That's what hospitality is, after all: anticipating the needs and desires of the people who choose to spend their time with us. The thirteen recipes ahead are abundant, festive, convivial and, in many cases, make-ahead friendly. And in at least one case—the Dumplings with Chile Crisp on page 200—preparing them can be a group activity.

So go ahead. Throw a party. Just don't be mad when your guests start abusing the plus-one button on the e-vite. You may need two Vegetarian Mushroom Wellingtons (page 192) when they get word of what you're cooking up.

VEGETARIAN MUSHROOM WELLINGTON
PAGE 192

MUSHROOM BOURGUIGNON
PAGE 196

CREAMED GREENS POTPIE
PAGE 198

DUMPLINGS WITH CHILE CRISP
PAGE 200

CHICKPEA, SPINACH AND FETA PIE
PAGE 202

KUKU SABZI (HERB AND SCALLION FRITTATA)
PAGE 204

ONE-POT VEGETABLE BIRYANI
PAGE 206

BORANI BANJAN (AFGHAN-STYLE EGGPLANT IN YOGURT)
PAGE 209

WHOLE ROASTED SQUASH WITH TOMATO-GINGER CHICKPEAS
PAGE 210

VEGETARIAN SHEPHERD'S PIE
PAGE 212

ASPARAGUS, GOAT CHEESE AND TARRAGON TART
PAGE 214

WHITE LASAGNA
PAGE 216

VEGAN SALTED MAPLE GINGER PIE
PAGE 219

VEGETARIAN MUSHROOM WELLINGTON

time 3 hours

yield 8 servings

Classic beef Wellington is a technical feat in which a tenderloin is coated with foie gras and mushroom duxelles, then wrapped in puff pastry and baked. This vegetarian version is less exacting yet just as impressive. Seared portobello mushrooms are layered with apple cider–caramelized onions and sautéed mushrooms, which are seasoned with soy sauce for flavor and bolstered with walnuts for texture. The rich mushroom filling is vegan, and the entire dish can easily be made vegan, too. Swap in vegan puff pastry, a butter substitute in the port reduction and caramelized onions, and an egg substitute for brushing the puff pastry. You can assemble and refrigerate the dish up to a day before baking it. Prepare the port reduction as the Wellington bakes, or skip it entirely and serve with cranberry sauce for a touch of tangy sweetness.

—Alexa Weibel

For the mushroom filling

4 large portobello mushrooms, each about 3 inches wide (8 to 10 ounces total)

½ cup plus 5 tablespoons olive oil

Kosher salt and black pepper

2 pounds mixed mushrooms, such as shiitake, oyster and cremini

Ice, for cooling

4 shallots, finely chopped (about 1 packed cup)

6 garlic cloves, finely chopped

2 tablespoons finely chopped fresh rosemary

⅓ cup port, or 1 to 2 tablespoons good-quality aged balsamic vinegar

2 tablespoons soy sauce

1 tablespoon fresh thyme leaves

1 cup finely chopped toasted walnuts (about 4 ounces)

For the onions

3 tablespoons unsalted butter

2 yellow onions, cut into ¼-inch rounds

¾ teaspoon light or dark brown sugar

1¼ teaspoons kosher salt

¾ teaspoon black pepper

1 cup apple cider or apple juice

1 tablespoon good-quality aged balsamic vinegar (optional)

For assembly

All-purpose flour, for dusting

1 (14-ounce) package frozen puff pastry, thawed

1 large egg, beaten

For the port reduction (optional)

2 tablespoons olive oil

1 large shallot, minced

2 garlic cloves, minced

2 teaspoons whole black peppercorns

1½ cups good-quality port

1½ cups vegetable stock, store-bought or homemade (page 224)

3 thyme sprigs

3 tablespoons unsalted butter

Kosher salt and black pepper

continued ›

"I made this for the vegans at my Friends Thanksgiving last night. I used a vegan egg, vegan puff pastry and vegan butter. Everyone LOVED it."
—Tara

VEGETARIAN MUSHROOM WELLINGTON, CONTINUED

1. Prepare the mushroom filling: Using moist paper towels, wipe the portobello mushrooms clean. Remove the stems, then slice off the excess rim that curls over the gills, creating a flat surface so the mushrooms can sear. Reserve the stems and scraps for use in Step 2. Brush the caps on both sides with 3 tablespoons oil and season generously with salt and pepper. In a large nonstick skillet, heat 2 tablespoons oil over medium-high heat and cook the mushrooms, gill side down, until caramelized, 5 minutes, then flip and cook another 5 minutes. Transfer to a wire rack, gill side down, to cool.
2. Separate and reserve any stems from the mixed mushrooms. (If using shiitakes, save their woody stems for another use.) Roughly chop about two-thirds of the mixed mushrooms, then working in batches, transfer the roughly chopped mushrooms to a food processor and pulse into ¼- to ½-inch pieces. Remove to a large bowl. By hand, finely chop the remaining mixed mushrooms and stems (including the reserved portobello stems and trimmings) into ¼-inch pieces. Add them to the bowl.
3. Prepare an ice water bath in a large bowl. (If preparing the mushrooms in advance, you can simply let the mixture cool to room temperature, then refrigerate.) Wipe out the skillet. Working in two batches, warm ¼ cup oil over medium-high heat. Add half the chopped mushrooms, shallots, garlic and rosemary, and season with salt and pepper. Cook, stirring occasionally, until caramelized and tender, about 10 minutes. Transfer to a medium bowl. Repeat with remaining ¼ cup oil and remaining mushrooms, shallots, garlic and rosemary. Return the first batch to the skillet. Add the port, soy sauce and thyme and cook over medium-high heat, stirring occasionally, until the liquid evaporates, 3 to 4 minutes. Return the mixture to the medium bowl and stir in the walnuts. Set the bowl into the ice water bath to cool, stirring occasionally, at least 20 minutes.
4. Prepare the onions: Wipe out the skillet, then melt the butter over medium heat. Add the onions, brown sugar, salt and pepper and cook, stirring occasionally, 5 minutes. Add the cider and cook, stirring occasionally, until the liquid evaporates and the onions are caramelized, about 15 minutes. Stir in the vinegar (if using), then let cool.
5. Assemble the Wellington: Heat the oven to 400 degrees. Place a large piece of parchment paper on your work surface and lightly dust it with flour. Unfold the thawed puff pastry on the parchment. Using a lightly floured rolling pin, roll out the pastry into a 13 by 16-inch rectangle. Transfer the parchment paper and puff pastry to a large sheet pan. Rotate so that one of the 16-inch sides is closest

to you. Arrange half the cooked mushroom mixture in a 4 by 10-inch strip in the center of the puff pastry, leaving a 1½-inch border at the ends. Arrange the caramelized onions in a 3-inch-wide strip on top. Lay the portobello mushrooms on top of the onions in a single line, stem side down. (If the portobellos are too large, square off edges.) Spoon remaining mushroom mixture on top, covering the portobello mushrooms, then gently pack the mushroom mixture to form an even layer on top, shaping it like a free-form meatloaf.

6. Lift one side of the puff pastry over the filling to almost completely cover it. Brush the surface of the puff pastry covering the mushrooms with beaten egg. Lift the remaining puff pastry flap over the egg-washed puff pastry, gently stretching it if needed to create a second layer of puff pastry on top, then gently press the top layer of pastry onto the lower layer to seal. Brush the insides of the short ends of the puff pastry and press to seal, tucking both sides underneath. Trim any parchment paper that extends beyond the sheet pan. (You can refrigerate the pastry for up to 1 day at this point.)

7. Brush the exposed puff pastry on top with remaining beaten egg. Decorate the top of the puff pastry as you like: Create a cross-hatch pattern by gently slicing through only the top layer in parallel lines, then cutting parallel lines in another direction. (Apply very little pressure, as you only want to cut through the top layer.) You can also slice small decorative vents (be sure to slice all the way through both layers of puff pastry), or top with additional strips or shapes made from egg-washed puff pastry. Bake until the puff pastry is deep golden and flaky, 45 to 50 minutes. Let cool slightly on the baking sheet, about 10 minutes.

8. While the Wellington bakes, prepare the optional port reduction: In a medium saucepan, heat the oil over medium heat. Add the shallot, garlic and peppercorns, and cook, stirring occasionally, 3 minutes. Add the port, stock and thyme; cook over medium-high heat until the sauce is glossy, 25 to 30 minutes. Strain the sauce. You should have about ½ cup. When ready to serve, reheat over medium heat, whisk in the butter, and season with salt and pepper.

9. To serve the mushroom Wellington, cut it crosswise into 8 even slabs. (Each slab will include a pretty cross-section showcasing the halved portobello mushroom in the center. This is considered the presentation side.) Serve each piece presentation side up. Pass with port reduction for drizzling on top.

MUSHROOM BOURGUIGNON

VEGAN

time 1 hour

yield 4 to 6 servings

Meaty mushrooms simmered with pearl onions, wine and carrots make for a rich, wintry Bourguignon-style stew. The quality of the stock here makes a big difference, so if you're not using homemade, buy a good brand. Mushroom or vegetable broth works well, especially because the whole dish is rounded out with tamari. For the best flavor, use as many kinds of mushrooms as you can get, and let them really brown when searing; that caramelization adds a lot of depth to the sauce. Maitake mushrooms give this a brisket-like texture, in a very good way.

—Melissa Clark

6 tablespoons butter or extra-virgin olive oil, plus more as needed

2 pounds mixed mushrooms, such as portobello, cremini, white button, shiitake or oyster, cut into 1-inch chunks (about 10 cups)

8 ounces pearl onions, larger ones cut in half (about 2 cups)

Salt and black pepper

1 large or 2 small leeks, white and light green parts, finely chopped (about 1½ cups)

2 carrots, thinly sliced

3 garlic cloves, 2 minced and 1 grated to a paste

1 tablespoon tomato paste

2½ tablespoons all-purpose flour

1½ cups dry red wine

1½ cups mushroom or vegetable broth, store-bought or homemade (page 224)

1 tablespoon tamari or soy sauce, plus more to taste

3 large thyme sprigs, or ½ teaspoon dried thyme

1 bay leaf

3 to 4 ounces chanterelle or oyster mushrooms, thinly sliced (about 1 cup)

Smoked paprika, for serving

Polenta or mashed potatoes, for serving

Chopped fresh flat-leaf parsley, for serving

1. In a large Dutch oven or heavy pot with a lid, melt 2 tablespoons butter over medium heat. Working in batches, stir in half the mixed mushrooms and half the pearl onions. (If they don't all fit in the pot in one layer, you might have to do this in three batches rather than two.) Without moving them around too much, cook the mushrooms until they are brown on one side, about 3 minutes. Stir and let them brown on the other side, 2 to 3 minutes more. Use a slotted spoon to transfer mushrooms and onions to a large bowl or plate and sprinkle with salt and pepper. Repeat with another 2 tablespoons butter and the remaining mushrooms and pearl onions, seasoning them as you go.
2. Reduce heat to medium-low. Add another 1 tablespoon butter to the pan. Add the leeks and carrots and sauté until the leeks turn lightly golden and start to soften, 5 minutes. Add the minced garlic and sauté for 1 minute longer. Stir in the tomato

paste and cook for 1 minute. Stir in the flour and cook, stirring, for 1 minute, then add the wine, broth, tamari, thyme and bay leaf, scraping up any brown bits at bottom of pot.

3. Add the reserved cooked mushrooms and pearl onions back to the pot and bring to a simmer. Partly cover and simmer on low heat until the carrots and onions are tender and the sauce is thick, 30 to 40 minutes. Taste and add more salt and tamari if needed. Stir in the grated garlic.
4. Just before serving, in a small skillet over high heat, melt ½ tablespoon butter. Add half the sliced chanterelle mushrooms and let cook undisturbed until crisp and brown on one side, 1 to 2 minutes. Flip and cook on the other side. Transfer to a plate and sprinkle with salt and smoked paprika. Repeat with remaining butter and mushrooms. Serve the mushroom Bourguignon over polenta, noodles or mashed potatoes, topped with the fried chanterelles and parsley.

CREAMED GREENS POTPIE

time 1 hour

yield 4 servings

This one-skillet, vegetarian potpie trades the traditional chicken filling for creamy, garlicky greens. Hearty greens turn silky in a mixture of heavy cream, garlic, shallot, thyme and Parmesan under a lid of flaky puff pastry. Using store-bought puff pastry in place of homemade pie crust ensures a perfect result every time. It also steers potpie into the weeknight-possible category. Greens and heavy cream require a good amount of salt to taste like their best selves, so taste and season well when the recipe says to do so.

—Ali Slagle

3 tablespoons unsalted butter

10 garlic cloves, thinly sliced

1 shallot, finely chopped

1 tablespoon fresh thyme leaves, or 1 teaspoon dried thyme

2½ pounds mixed hearty greens, such as kale, spinach, mustard greens or collard greens, tough stems discarded and leaves torn into large pieces

Salt and black pepper

1 tablespoon all-purpose flour, plus more for rolling

2 cups heavy cream

1 teaspoon hot sauce

½ cup freshly grated Parmesan

1 sheet frozen puff pastry, thawed

1 large egg, beaten

1. Heat the oven to 400 degrees. Line a baking sheet with parchment paper or foil and set aside.
2. In a medium oven-safe skillet, melt the butter over medium heat. Add the garlic, shallot and thyme and cook, stirring occasionally, until softened but not browned, 5 to 6 minutes.
3. Add a handful of the greens and season lightly with salt and pepper. Using tongs, toss the greens in the butter until wilted. Repeat, making sure to season each batch, until all the greens are added and wilted. (They will all fit eventually.)
4. Stir in the flour until it disappears into the greens, then add the cream and hot sauce and stir well to combine. Bring to a simmer, then remove from heat and stir in the Parmesan. Season to taste with salt and pepper.
5. Lightly flour your work surface (or the bottom of another baking sheet) and rolling pin. Roll and trim the puff pastry into a 12-inch round. If you find the pastry contracts when you roll it, give it a few minutes between each roll to relax a little.
6. Transfer the skillet to the lined baking sheet. Drape the puff pastry over the skillet, leaving about a ½-inch overhang. (Trim any excess of more than an inch.) Brush with the egg, then cut four large slits into the pastry. Bake until the pastry is puffed and golden brown, about 10 minutes. Reduce heat to 375 degrees

and bake until the pastry is cooked through and the filling is bubbling, 30 to 35 minutes. (If the pastry is getting too dark, cover with foil.) Let sit for a few minutes before diving in.

DUMPLINGS WITH CHILE CRISP

VEGAN

time 1 hour

yield about 35 dumplings

Great dumplings are as much about texture as taste, and these double the welcome contrast of tenderness and crunch. Simultaneously fried and steamed in a covered skillet, the wrappers develop a crackling brown base, while the tops become delicately chewy. Inside, the crunch of spicy chile crisp punctuates soft tofu and greens. Wringing the water from the tofu and greens allows them to absorb more of the soy sauce and chile crisp and ensures the filling doesn't end up watery or bland. Another benefit to this vegan filling is the ability to taste it raw and adjust the seasonings before wrapping.

—Genevieve Ko

8 ounces firm tofu, cut into ¼-inch slices

6 ounces spinach, watercress or baby bok choy, finely chopped (about 3 cups)

3 ounces garlic chives or scallions, thinly sliced (about 1 cup)

1 teaspoon kosher salt, such as Diamond Crystal

2 celery stalks, finely chopped (about ½ cup)

1 tablespoon soy sauce, plus more for serving

1 tablespoon chile crisp, plus more for serving

35 round dumpling wrappers, store-bought or homemade

Grapeseed oil or other neutral oil, for frying

Chinese black vinegar or unseasoned rice vinegar, for serving

Sesame oil, for serving

1. Arrange the tofu slices in a single layer on a clean kitchen towel or between double layers of paper towels. Roll up tightly, as if rolling a sleeping bag, then squeeze over the sink to remove as much liquid as possible. Let stand 10 minutes for the tofu to continue releasing liquid. If the towel gets soaked, transfer the tofu to another dry towel.
2. Toss together the spinach, chives and salt in a colander. Let stand for 10 minutes, then squeeze the greens over the sink to release as much liquid as possible. Transfer the greens mixture to a large bowl. Add the drained tofu, crumbling it into bits, then mix evenly with the greens. Add the celery, soy sauce and chile crisp and stir until evenly mixed. Taste and add more soy sauce and chile crisp, if you'd like. The filling should be very flavorful because the wrappers are not seasoned at all.
3. Set up a dumpling assembly line with the bowl of filling, the wrappers and a small bowl of water. Using a dessert spoon or other small spoon, scoop a mound of filling, then press it against the side of the bowl to form a tiny football. Place the filling in the center of a wrapper. Use your fingertip to dampen the edges of the wrapper with water. Bring together the sides over the filling to enclose in a half-

"I have never gotten so many compliments on my dumplings!"

—LF Chung

moon. Pinch the center, then press the edges to seal, pleating decoratively if you'd like. Sit the dumpling upright on your work surface. Repeat with the remaining filling and wrappers. Cook immediately or freeze in a single layer on a rimmed baking sheet until solid, then transfer to airtight containers and freeze for up to 3 months.

4. You can cook as many or as few dumplings at a time as you'd like. Choose your pan size accordingly: an 8-inch skillet will fit 8 to 10 dumplings; a 10-inch skillet will fit 14 to 16 dumplings. When ready to cook, coat a well-seasoned cast-iron or nonstick skillet with a lid with a thin layer of neutral oil. Arrange the dumplings in the pan, pleated side up, spacing ⅓ inch apart and filling the pan. Add enough cold water to the pan to come ⅓ inch up the sides (about ¼ cup for an 8-inch pan; ½ cup for a 10-inch pan).
5. Cover the skillet and cook over medium heat until the rapid firecracker popping diminishes to a steady, low crackle, indicating that all the water has evaporated, about 10 minutes. Uncover and check to see if the bottoms are browned and the dough is slightly translucent all the way to the top. If so, remove from heat. If not, cook, uncovered, 1 to 2 minutes longer. Let stand for a minute so the dumplings release from the skillet naturally. Transfer to a plate, browned side up. Make your own dipping sauce with any combination of soy sauce, chile crisp, vinegar and sesame oil and enjoy with the hot dumplings.

CHICKPEA, SPINACH AND FETA PIE

time 50 minutes

yield 4 to 6 servings

Bringing together inspiration from two great Greek pies, spanakopita (spinach and feta) and prasopita (leek), this one-skillet dish also incorporates chickpeas for extra heartiness. Don't let looks deceive you—this elegant pie couldn't be easier to make. There's no need to stress about torn or dry phyllo sheets here; in fact, the pastry is deliberately broken and scrunched up into jagged, clumpy pieces that are simply plopped on top of the pie. When baked, the craggy pastry becomes extra shattery and crisp—and visually arresting. (This forgiving recipe also welcomes any leftover pastry that may seem dry or past its prime.) This is a pie for all occasions, easy enough for weeknight cooking but special enough for entertaining.

—Hetty Lui McKinnon

2 large leeks (about 1 pound), halved lengthwise and thinly sliced

9 tablespoons extra-virgin olive oil

Salt and black pepper

3 garlic cloves, finely chopped

5 ounces baby spinach

1 (15-ounce) can chickpeas, drained

7 ounces feta, crumbled

1 lemon, zested and juiced (3 to 4 tablespoons)

1 cup chopped fresh dill

8 to 10 frozen phyllo pastry sheets (about 10 ounces), thawed

Toasted white sesame or nigella seeds, for topping (optional)

Lemon wedges, for serving

1. Heat the oven to 375 degrees.
2. Place the sliced leeks in a colander and rinse them well, rubbing to loosen any dirt. Rinse again and drain well. (There is no need to dry them; the residual water helps cook the leeks.)
3. Heat a medium oven-safe skillet over medium-high heat for 1 to 2 minutes. Add 2 tablespoons oil along with the leeks (the skillet will look overfilled, but the leeks will cook down a lot). Season generously with salt and pepper and cook, stirring occasionally, until the leeks are wilted, 3 to 5 minutes.
4. Add the garlic and the spinach, a few handfuls at a time, adding more as it wilts, and toss until the leaves have all softened. Turn off heat and add the chickpeas, feta, lemon zest, lemon juice and dill. Taste and season generously with salt and pepper.
5. Place the phyllo sheets in a large bowl and drizzle with 5 tablespoons olive oil. Scrunch and massage the oil into the sheets; the sheets will crumble and clump and that is fine. Arrange the pastry clumps on top of the leeks and spinach,

"My partner and I both LOVED this. Don't fuss about the amount of spinach, eyeball it, it's a recipe that can accommodate variation."

—**Sam B**

covering them completely. Drizzle the top with remaining 2 tablespoons oil and scatter the sesame or nigella seeds over (if using).

6. Bake until the top is golden and crispy, 30 to 35 minutes. Let cool for 5 to 10 minutes. Serve with lemon wedges on the side.

KUKU SABZI (HERB AND SCALLION FRITTATA)

time 1 hour

yield 6 servings

Packed with an abundance of fresh herbs, kuku is a frittata-like Persian dish with many regional and household variations. Kuku sabzi is the most herb-forward of these, allowing the greens to take center stage. While kuku is often flipped to brown on both sides, this recipe skips that step and allows the egg on top to set under the broiler, which helps retain the kuku's vibrant green color. Some families mix in walnuts or tart dried barberries for added texture and flavor, but this rendition keeps it simple, letting the herbs shine. Kuku is traditionally served with flatbread and can be enjoyed warm, at room temperature or even cold. For a perfect bite, wrap it in lavash with a dollop of yogurt, slices of salty feta and crisp radishes, which balance the richness with bright, fresh flavors.

—Andy Baraghani

3 bunches cilantro

3 bunches flat-leaf parsley

2 bunches dill

2 bunches scallions (about 10), trimmed and thinly sliced

1 tablespoon dried fenugreek leaves

1½ teaspoons kosher salt, or ¾ teaspoon fine sea salt

1 teaspoon black pepper

1 teaspoon ground turmeric

5 large eggs

¼ cup canola or grapeseed oil

Barbari, lavash, pita or other flatbread, for serving

Torshi (Persian pickles) or other savory pickled cucumbers, for serving

Plain yogurt, for serving

1. When preparing such a large quantity of herbs, wash them in batches to ensure any lingering sand or dirt is fully removed. Trim off the thick stems of the cilantro, parsley and dill (about 4 inches from the bottom). Grab a large handful of the herbs and, using a chef's knife, finely chop. Repeat with remaining herbs until you have about 4½ cups total. Transfer the chopped herbs to a large bowl and add the scallions.
2. Using your fingertips, pinch and crush the fenugreek, sprinkling it over the herb mixture. Add the salt, pepper and turmeric. Add the eggs and use a fork to break the yolks, then mix until fully incorporated. (It may seem like not enough eggs, but you want just enough to bind the mixture.)
3. Place an oven rack 5 inches from the heat source and heat the broiler.
4. Pour the oil into a 10-inch nonstick oven-safe skillet with a lid and place it over medium heat. When the oil begins to shimmer, give the kuku batter a final mix and then scrape it into the skillet. Using a spatula, spread the batter to the sides of the skillet. Cover and cook, rotating the skillet to ensure it cooks evenly,

"Just in time for Nowruz this is the ultimate version of this dish for the beautiful season of abundance and joy, spring!"

—MjinNH

until the bottom has set and turned a very dark green, almost brown color, 10 to 12 minutes.

5. Remove the skillet from heat and uncover. The top of the kuku will still be a touch wet but very green. Transfer the skillet to the oven and broil, watching carefully, until the top is set, anywhere from 1 to 4 minutes. Slide the kuku onto a platter or cutting board. Let cool for 10 minutes before slicing. Serve with flatbread, pickles and yogurt.

ONE-POT VEGETABLE BIRYANI

time 1 hour

yield 4 to 6 servings

Vegetable biryani may be the underdog of biryanis since it's often overshadowed by meatier varieties. But like other formidable yet unsung dishes, this one's adaptability helps it hold its own. Recipes vary across South Asia: Hyderabadi versions are known for their fieriness, while milder, nuttier variations dominate northern regions. This one falls somewhere in the middle. Use any vegetables you have, such as nutty cauliflower, sweet peas and crunchy carrots. Nuts and fresh or dried fruits add a confetti of flavors and textures. This recipe skips the layering typically called for in favor of conveniently stirring everything together. Luckily, using fewer dishes doesn't compromise flavor.

—Zainab Shah

2 cups basmati rice

¼ cup ghee or any neutral oil

1 dried bay leaf

2 whole star anise (optional)

4 whole cloves

4 cardamom pods

4 fresh Thai green chiles or green finger chiles

1 red onion, finely chopped

1 tablespoon ginger paste or freshly grated peeled ginger

1 tablespoon garlic paste or freshly grated garlic

½ teaspoon turmeric powder

2 teaspoons Kashmiri or other red chile powder

1 plum tomato, finely chopped

½ cup chopped cilantro leaves

½ cup chopped mint leaves

1 medium carrot, thinly sliced

1 small potato, peeled and finely diced

1 cup small cauliflower florets

½ cup frozen peas, thawed

½ cup fresh or frozen cut green beans

½ cup full-fat plain Greek yogurt

2 tablespoons fine sea salt

1 teaspoon garam masala

1 tablespoon fresh lemon juice

2½ cups unsalted vegetable stock, store-bought or homemade (page 224), or water

3 lemon slices

½ cup pomegranate seeds (optional)

¼ cup toasted or fried cashews halves (optional)

1. Rinse the rice, cover with cold water in a small bowl and soak for 20 minutes. Meanwhile, in a large pot with a lid, melt the ghee over medium heat, 30 to 45 seconds. Add the bay leaf, star anise, cloves, cardamom and chiles and fry until fragrant, about 30 seconds. Add onion and fry, stirring often, until it starts to turn golden brown, about 5 minutes.
2. Add the ginger and garlic and continue frying and stirring until the raw smell dissipates, about 1 minute. Add the turmeric and chile powder and stir for

> “Was really stumped on what to make as a veg main for family thanksgiving and this was IT! Came out so delicious and will def make this again.”
>
> **—Vanessa**

30 seconds to toast (don’t let them burn). Add the tomato and 2 tablespoons water. Add ¼ cup cilantro and ¼ cup mint. Continue stirring until the tomato starts to break down, about 5 minutes.

3. Add the carrot, potato, cauliflower, peas, green beans, yogurt and salt. Cook, stirring occasionally, for 5 minutes, until the ingredients are incorporated.
4. Drain the rice and add to the pot, along with the lemon juice and garam masala. Stir until everything is evenly mixed. Add the stock and stir. Cover and cook over medium heat for 5 minutes.
5. Uncover and stir. Add remaining ¼ cup cilantro, ¼ cup mint and the lemon slices. Cover and cook over low heat for 20 minutes. Turn off heat and let stand for 15 minutes. Fluff the rice, then garnish with pomegranate seeds and cashews (if using).

"So refreshing for summer and it didn't need to be served immediately, which is helpful for dinner parties."

—Catherine B.

BORANI BANJAN (AFGHAN-STYLE EGGPLANT IN YOGURT)

time 35 minutes

yield 4 servings

In traditional Afghan borani banjan, an appetizer or vegetable side, eggplant slices are soaked in salted water for 20 to 30 minutes, drained and dried, then simmered in a spiced tomato sauce before being served in layers of garlicky yogurt. This version significantly simplifies the preparation without compromising its appeal: crispy, caramelized eggplant; creamy, garlicky yogurt; sweet and sour tomatoes; and juicy, bright pomegranate seeds. No soaking or simmering here, just quick pan-frying and layering for the same effect in about 30 minutes. Go back for seconds of a dish that tastes even better cold.

—Zainab Shah

1 cup full-fat plain Greek or Indian yogurt

1 garlic clove, grated

Kosher salt, such as Diamond Crystal

½ to 1 cup vegetable oil

4 Japanese or Indian eggplants (see Tip), or 1 globe eggplant, cut into ¼-inch-thick rounds

3 ripe plum tomatoes, chopped

½ teaspoon Kashmiri or other red chile powder (optional)

2 tablespoons pomegranate seeds

4 to 6 small fresh mint leaves

1. In a small bowl, mix together the yogurt, garlic, ½ teaspoon salt and 2 tablespoons water. Place in the fridge to chill and develop a garlicky flavor.
2. Line a tray or large plate with paper towels. In a large frying pan, heat ⅓ cup oil over high heat. (The eggplant slices should be submerged about halfway in the oil while frying.) When the oil is hot, working in batches to avoid overcrowding, add the eggplant slices in a single layer and fry 1 to 2 minutes on each side, until starting to caramelize. Transfer to the prepared tray. Pat dry with a paper towel or clean kitchen towel to remove any excess oil and preserve the eggplant's crisp texture, then season with salt as desired. Repeat with the remaining eggplant, adding more oil between batches as necessary.
3. To the same pan, add the tomatoes, ½ teaspoon salt, 2 tablespoons water and the chile powder (if using). Cook over high heat until the tomatoes start to break down, about 5 minutes.
4. To serve, spread the chilled yogurt mixture in a large shallow dish. Add the eggplant in a single layer on top, then scatter the tomato over the eggplant (see Tip). Finish with the pomegranate seeds and mint.

Tips

Indian eggplants tend to be round and about 2 inches in diameter, with thinner skin. These eggplants have a milder flavor and creamier texture than globe eggplants when cooked.

If multiple layers are preferred (the traditional way), use half of the yogurt, eggplant and tomato for the first layer and create a second layer with the second half of the elements.

WHOLE ROASTED SQUASH WITH TOMATO-GINGER CHICKPEAS

time about 3 hours

yield 6 to 8 servings

With creamy squash, sticky chickpeas and tangy yogurt, this vegetarian sheet-pan feast easily serves a crowd. The method here doesn't bother with cutting rock-hard raw winter squash. Instead, roast the squash whole until you can rip them apart into wedges. Meanwhile, chickpeas, tomatoes, olive oil and a warming combination of cinnamon, ginger and marjoram cook down until the chickpeas are buttery-soft and the tomatoes caramelized. Accompany with yogurt and perhaps salad greens dressed with lemon or lime juice. To make ahead, refrigerate the cooked squash pieces, chickpeas and yogurt separately for up to 4 days. Reheat the squash and chickpeas covered in a low-temperature oven or serve at room temperature. To make vegan, add lemon or lime juice to nondairy yogurt until tangy.

—Ali Slagle

3 (15-ounce) cans chickpeas, drained

⅔ cup extra-virgin olive oil, plus more for drizzling

3 (14-ounce) cans diced tomatoes with their juices

¾ teaspoon ground cinnamon

4 marjoram sprigs or 3 oregano sprigs

2½ tablespoons finely chopped peeled fresh ginger

Salt and black pepper

2 (3- to 4-pound) kabocha, butternut or koginut squash

1 (5-ounce) container full-fat plain Greek yogurt (¾ cup)

Marjoram or oregano leaves, for garnish

1. Place racks in the upper and lower thirds of the oven and heat the oven to 300 degrees. On a sheet pan, stir together the chickpeas, oil, tomatoes, cinnamon, marjoram sprigs and 2 tablespoons chopped ginger. Season with salt and pepper and spread in an even layer.
2. Scrub the squash—the skin is perfectly edible—and prick in a few places with a paring knife. Transfer to a large oven-safe skillet, baking dish or second sheet pan (line with foil for easier cleanup) and coat lightly with oil. Season with salt and pepper.
3. Bake the squash on the bottom rack and the chickpeas on the upper rack until a knife slides easily through the squash, and the chickpeas and tomatoes are dark red and thick like jam, 2 to 2½ hours, stirring the chickpeas occasionally.
4. Meanwhile, stir remaining ½ tablespoon ginger into the yogurt. Stir in water, a tablespoon at a time, until thin enough to drizzle, then season to taste with salt and pepper. Refrigerate until ready to serve.

"This makes for a perfect winter supper—you have the long, slow cooking to warm up your kitchen and then the squash/chickpea supper to warm you again."

—Clare C.

5. Discard the herb sprigs, then season the chickpeas to taste with salt and pepper. When the squash are cool enough to handle, cut or tear into big pieces, then scoop out and discard the stems, seeds and stringy bits. Season the squash with salt and pepper. Transfer the squash to a platter flesh side up, then top with the chickpeas, some of the ginger yogurt and a sprinkle of marjoram leaves. Serve remaining yogurt alongside.

VEGETARIAN SHEPHERD'S PIE

time 1 hour 45 minutes

yield 4 to 6 servings

French green lentils (Puy lentils) make a hearty base for this vegetarian shepherd's pie. They may be slightly harder to find than other lentils, but they're worth the extra effort. Unlike brown or red lentils, green lentils retain their shape and texture after cooking, which means they stand up well to a long simmer and this rich potato topping. Store-bought vegetable stock can vary greatly, so be sure to buy one with a pleasant flavor that isn't too sweet.

—Samantha Seneviratne

For the topping

Kosher salt, such as Diamond Crystal

2 pounds russet potatoes, peeled and quartered (about 3 large)

6 tablespoons unsalted butter

½ cup whole milk

½ cup sour cream

½ cup packed grated Parmesan (optional)

Black pepper

For the filling

¾ cup French green lentils

4 thyme sprigs

1 teaspoon kosher salt, plus more for seasoning

3½ cups vegetable broth, store-bought or homemade (page 224)

4 tablespoons butter

8 ounces sliced mixed mushrooms, such as button, cremini and shiitake

1 large leek, white part only, thinly sliced (about 1½ cups)

2 medium carrots, diced (about 1 cup)

2 garlic cloves, minced

Freshly ground black pepper

2 tablespoons tomato paste

2 tablespoons all-purpose flour

1 cup frozen peas, thawed

1 to 2 teaspoons fresh lemon juice

1. Start the topping: In a large pot, bring 4 quarts of water and 2 tablespoons salt to a boil over high heat. Add the potatoes and boil until soft, 15 to 20 minutes. A knife should slide in with almost no resistance.
2. Meanwhile, prepare the filling: In a 10-inch oven-safe skillet with high sides and a lid or an enameled cast-iron braiser, bring the lentils, thyme, salt and 2 cups broth to a simmer over medium-high heat. Reduce heat, partially cover, and cook until the lentils are tender and most of the liquid is absorbed, about 20 minutes. Transfer to a small bowl.
3. Finish the topping: In a small saucepan, heat the butter and milk over medium heat until butter melts. (Or you can place the butter and milk in a microwave-safe bowl and microwave in increments.) Drain the potatoes well and return to the large pot. Using a masher or a ricer, mash hot potatoes until smooth. Mix in

"I made this as a vegan main for Christmas by using non-dairy milk, vegan butter and vegan sour cream. It turned out excellent and everyone, meat lovers included, devoured it!"

—Olivia

the hot butter mixture and sour cream just until blended. Stir in ¼ cup cheese (if using). Season to taste with salt and pepper. Cover and set aside.

4. Finish the filling: Heat the oven to 375 degrees. Melt the butter in the 10-inch skillet over medium-high heat. Add the mushrooms and cook, stirring often with a wooden spoon, until deep golden brown, 8 to 10 minutes. Reduce heat to medium and add the leek, carrots and garlic. Continue to cook until tender, another 10 minutes. Season to taste with salt and pepper. Add the tomato paste and cook, stirring, until well combined, another 2 to 3 minutes. Sprinkle the flour over the mixture, stir and cook for 1 minute. Add remaining 1½ cups broth, the cooked lentils and thawed peas and cook until thickened. Remove the thyme sprigs and stir in the lemon juice.
5. Top the mixture with dollops of the mashed potatoes, then spread them out over the top. (Or transfer the lentil mixture to a 3-quart casserole dish, spread into an even layer, then top with potatoes.) Sprinkle with remaining cheese (if using). Transfer to the oven. If the mixture is at the top edges of your pan, set a foil-lined baking sheet underneath the pan to catch any drips. Bake the pie until the potatoes have begun to brown and the edges are bubbling, about 30 minutes. Let stand at room temperature for 15 minutes before serving.

ASPARAGUS, GOAT CHEESE AND TARRAGON TART

time 1 hour

yield 6 to 8 servings

Because you don't have to make your own crust, this gorgeous asparagus-striped tart is so easy it almost feels like cheating. But it's not. It's simple yet stunning, effortlessly chic and company-ready. With so few ingredients, each one makes an impact; be sure to buy a good all-butter brand of puff pastry. If you can manage to serve this tart warm, within an hour of baking, it will be at its absolute best, with crisp pastry that shatters into buttery bits when you bite down and still-runny cheese. But it's also excellent a few hours later, should you want to get all your baking done before your guests arrive. If tarragon isn't your favorite herb, you can use chives, basil or mint instead. And if you can manage to trim all the asparagus to the same length, this tart will be especially neat and orderly looking.

—Melissa Clark

4 ounces soft goat cheese, at room temperature (about 1 cup)

1 large egg, lightly beaten, at room temperature

1 large garlic clove, finely grated or minced

1½ tablespoons chopped fresh tarragon leaves, plus more for serving

½ tablespoon finely grated lemon zest

½ teaspoon fine sea salt, plus more for sprinkling

Pinch of freshly grated nutmeg

1 cup crème fraîche, at room temperature

All-purpose flour, for dusting

1 (9- to 14-ounce; brands vary) sheet or square all-butter puff pastry, thawed if frozen

8 ounces thin asparagus, woody ends trimmed

Extra-virgin olive oil

2 tablespoons grated Parmesan

Freshly ground black pepper

Red pepper flakes (optional)

1½ ounces Parmesan, shaved with a vegetable peeler (about ½ cup)

1. Heat the oven to 425 degrees. In a medium bowl, use a fork or a wooden spoon to mash together the goat cheese, egg, garlic, tarragon, lemon zest, salt and nutmeg until smooth. Switch to a whisk and beat in the crème fraîche until smooth.
2. Line a cookie sheet with parchment paper. Lightly flour your work surface, then roll out the puff pastry into a 13 by 11-inch rectangle about ⅛ inch thick. Transfer the dough to the prepared cookie sheet. With a sharp knife, lightly score a ½-inch border around the edges of the puff pastry.
3. Spread the crème fraîche mixture evenly inside the scored border. Line up the asparagus spears on top, and brush them with oil. Sprinkle some salt and the grated Parmesan over the asparagus.

Tip

You can assemble the tart 1 day in advance, but reserve the sprinkling of salt and grated Parmesan until right before baking. Loosely cover the tart with foil and store it in the refrigerator until it's time to bake.

"I've made this several times as an appetizer and it always gets rave reviews."

—**Debra Mott**

4. Bake until the pastry is puffed and golden, 25 to 30 minutes. Let it cool on the cookie sheet for at least 15 minutes or up to 4 hours before serving. Then sprinkle with black pepper, red pepper flakes (if using), the shaved Parmesan and some tarragon. Drizzle a little oil on top.

WHITE LASAGNA

time 3 hours 15 minutes

yield 6 main course or 12 appetizer or side-dish servings

Made without Bolognese or tomato sauce, a white lasagna is a celebration of pasta and vegetables bound together by creamy béchamel. This version, brimming with herbs, spinach, asparagus and peas, is an ode to spring, like a baked pasta primavera in its richest form. Serve it in small squares as a first or pasta course, as it's served in Italy, or in more substantial slabs as a meatless main course. It's a bit of a project, so if you want to work ahead, you can make the béchamel up to a week in advance and store it in the refrigerator. The baked lasagna can also be made ahead and refrigerated for up to two days. Reheat, covered, in a 350-degree oven for 30 to 45 minutes.

—Melissa Clark

For the béchamel

¼ cup unsalted butter, plus more for greasing

⅓ cup all-purpose flour

4 cups whole milk, plus more if needed

1 teaspoon fine sea salt or table salt, plus more to taste

¼ teaspoon freshly grated nutmeg

1 bay leaf

½ cup grated Parmesan

2 garlic cloves, finely grated or minced

For the filling

3 tablespoons extra-virgin olive oil

1 bunch asparagus, woody ends trimmed, cut into ¾-inch pieces

Fine sea salt or table salt and freshly ground black pepper

½ cup frozen peas (no need to thaw)

1 cup mixed fresh soft herbs, such as parsley, chives, basil and dill, finely chopped, plus more for garnish

2 leeks, white and light green parts, thinly sliced

1 teaspoon fennel seeds

¼ teaspoon red pepper flakes

8 ounces baby spinach or other baby greens, such as kale or arugula (about 8 cups), chopped

1 lemon, zested and juiced

32 ounces whole-milk ricotta (about 4 cups)

1¼ cups grated Parmesan

¾ cup grated Pecorino Romano

12 ounces dried lasagna noodles (about 12 noodles), or substitute the same amount of no-boil, oven-ready or fresh noodles; all will work

8 ounces whole-milk mozzarella, thinly sliced

continued ›

"We thought it was just perfect and great for feeding a crowd in spring."

—tory

WHITE LASAGNA, CONTINUED

1. Heat the oven to 400 degrees. Grease a 9-by-13-inch baking pan with a little butter.
2. Make the béchamel: In a large saucepan, melt the butter over medium heat. Add the flour and whisk until combined. Cook for 4 to 5 minutes, or until pale golden. Gradually whisk in the milk, a little at a time so that the sauce does not clump. Add the salt, nutmeg and bay leaf. Gently bring to a simmer and let cook for 9 to 12 minutes, whisking often, until the béchamel is thick but still pourable. Stir in the Parmesan and garlic. Taste and add more salt if needed.
3. While the béchamel is cooking, prepare the filling: Place a large skillet over medium-high heat and add 1 tablespoon oil. Let it heat until it thins out, about 30 seconds, then add the asparagus and sauté, shaking the pan, until crisp-tender, about 4 minutes. Season with salt and black pepper, then transfer to a medium bowl and stir in the peas and 2 tablespoons herbs.
4. Add the remaining 2 tablespoons oil to the pan and heat until the oil thins out, about 30 seconds. Add the leeks, fennel seeds, red pepper flakes and ¾ teaspoon salt. Sauté until the leeks are tender and golden at the edges, 4 to 6 minutes. Working in batches if needed, add the spinach and remaining herbs and sauté until the spinach is very tender and the pan is very dry, about 10 minutes. Stir in the lemon zest and juice. Taste and add more salt if needed; the mixture should be well seasoned.
5. Transfer the spinach mixture to a large bowl. Stir in the ricotta and ¾ cup each Parmesan and Pecorino (save the remaining Parmesan for the top). Taste and add more salt if needed.
6. Remove the bay leaf from the béchamel, then ladle some of the sauce into the bottom of the prepared baking pan to just cover. Arrange noodles in an even layer over the sauce, breaking or cutting them to fit as needed. Ladle a little more béchamel on top of the noodles, spreading to cover the surface. Add half of the ricotta mixture, spreading evenly, then sprinkle half of the asparagus-pea mixture on top. Add another layer of noodles, followed by béchamel, the remaining ricotta mixture and the remaining asparagus-pea mixture. Top with the mozzarella. Add a third and final layer of noodles (don't worry if you don't end up using them all) and cover with the remaining béchamel. Sprinkle with the remaining ½ cup Parmesan.
7. Cover the pan with foil and place on a rimmed baking sheet to catch any drips. Bake for 30 minutes, then remove foil and continue to bake for another 30 to 40 minutes, or until golden brown and bubbling on top. (If the top is still pale, you can run the lasagna under the broiler for 1 to 3 minutes.) Let sit for 20 to 30 minutes before serving.

VEGAN SALTED MAPLE GINGER PIE

VEGAN

time 3 hours 20 minutes, plus overnight chilling

yield 8 to 10 servings

Like a ginger ale at 30,000 feet, this zippy pie might be just the thing to settle your stomach after a feast. Ample salt in both the crust and the filling helps this vegan dessert avoid saccharine territory. Starchy, mild Japanese sweet potato provides plenty of structure to the egg-free custard without competing with assertive fresh ginger or warming maple, but a sweet potato pie this is not. This pie is a treat for real ginger lovers, but if you're on the fence, feel free to adjust the quantity of grated ginger (and maple extract while you're at it, see Tip) to your preference. The beauty of a vegan pie is that you can taste and adjust the filling as you go.

—Tanya Sichynsky

For the filling

½ cup/75 grams whole raw cashews

1 (8-ounce/226-gram) Japanese or orange sweet potato, scrubbed

⅓ cup/105 milliliters pure maple syrup

1 (16-ounce) package silken tofu, excess liquid poured off

½ cup/110 grams packed dark brown sugar

2 tablespoons coconut oil, room temperature

2 tablespoons freshly grated ginger

1 tablespoon cornstarch

1 teaspoon maple extract (see Tip)

1 teaspoon kosher salt, such as Diamond Crystal

For the crust

2 tablespoons melted coconut oil, plus more for greasing

7 ounces/200 grams gingersnap cookies (check label if you follow a vegan or gluten-free diet)

1½ cups/145 grams pecan halves

2 tablespoons dark brown sugar

¾ teaspoon kosher salt, such as Diamond Crystal

For the topping

½ cup/50 grams pecan halves, roughly chopped

2 tablespoons dark brown sugar

2 tablespoons flour (all-purpose, almond or gluten-free)

¼ teaspoon kosher salt, such as Diamond Crystal

1 tablespoon coconut oil, at room temperature

continued ›

VEGAN SALTED MAPLE GINGER PIE, CONTINUED

1. Start the filling: Add the cashews to a small bowl, amply cover with water and let sit for 2 hours, until very soft.
2. Meanwhile, fill a saucepan with an inch or two of water and place a steamer basket inside. Bring to a boil over high heat, then add the sweet potato to the basket and cover. Reduce heat to medium-low and steam until tender and a fork meets no resistance, 40 to 50 minutes. Halve the sweet potato. When the sweet potato is cool enough to handle, scoop the flesh into a bowl and mash. (You should have about 1 cup.)
3. While the sweet potato steams, make the crust: Heat the oven to 350 degrees. With a paper towel or your hands, grease a 9-inch springform pan with coconut oil.
4. In a food processor, pulse the gingersnaps and pecans until finely ground. Add the coconut oil, brown sugar and salt, and pulse until the mixture looks like damp sand, scraping down the sides as needed.
5. Transfer the crumb mixture to the prepared pan and wipe out the food processor (no need for a thorough wash). Using your fingers or the bottom of a dry measuring cup, evenly press the crumbs into the bottom and about an inch up the sides of the pan. Bake for about 10 minutes, until firm and lightly toasted. Let the crust cool while you blend the filling.
6. Finish the filling: Drain the cashews and add to the food processor along with the maple syrup and blend until silky. Add the sweet potato, tofu, brown sugar, coconut oil, ginger, cornstarch, maple extract and salt. Blend until silky, stopping to scrape down the sides of the bowl as needed. Pulse a few more times to combine.
7. Pour the filling into the cooled crust and bake for 25 minutes.
8. Meanwhile, make the topping: In a small bowl, mix the pecans, brown sugar, flour and salt until combined. Dot with the coconut oil and then use your hands to squeeze and press the mixture into clumps, distributing the coconut oil throughout. Set aside.
9. Remove the pie from the oven and sprinkle the topping in a ring around the edges. Return to the oven and bake for 25 minutes more, until the filling is lightly golden and set and the topping is fragrant and toasted. Let cool on a wire rack until the pan is cool to the touch, then transfer to the refrigerator to cool completely, at least 5 hours and ideally overnight. To serve, gently release the sides of the pan and cut into slices, cleaning the knife between cuts as needed.

Tip

Maple extract gives this pie a subtle but irresistible pancakey aroma. (Add it to other baked goods or whipped cream!) Products can vary in intensity. Start by adding ¼ teaspoon to the filling and taste as you go, increasing in ¼-teaspoon increments. Anything labeled "maple flavor concentrate" or "maple oil" is more highly concentrated than extract; start with a small amount and adjust to your liking.

"Oh my goodness, it was fantastic. The saltiness . . . the unapologetic gingeriness. I want a whole one all to myself."

—Diane M.

CHAPTER 8

VEG ESSENTIALS

I remember the first pot of beans I made with eidetic clarity. A college student, I'd set out to emulate the Cuban-style frijoles negros I grew up eating: a couple cans of black beans, garlic and onion, oregano. Seemed simple enough. But they lacked the savory depth I knew. Disappointed with my result, I called my mother. A splash of red wine vinegar was the secret that hadn't yet reached my ears.

It wasn't until the pandemic that I made my first pot of dried beans. (Yes, I also fed a sourdough starter and whipped instant coffee and regrew scallion stubs on the windowsill. I got Bingo.) This time around, I turned to the internet. The long-simmering nature of a perfect pot of beans intimidated me: Must I soak them? With my first pot, I did. But Melissa Clark's recipe for a Big Pot of Beans gave me permission to adapt a recipe to my life: "If you don't have time, you can skip this step," she writes on page 227. Ahh. Embrace the soak for quicker-cooking beans and easier digestion, but don't beat yourself up if you forget. Just don't skip the aromatics.

In this chapter, you'll find that pot of beans alongside seven other recipes that are more method than meal, the results you hope for when you punch in a "how do I make X?" online query on your phone while standing in the kitchen. You don't need Google or ChatGPT or Reddit. You have Melissa.

These are the sort of building blocks that make cooking with more vegetables and less meat not only approachable but fun and creative. Want to perk up crisper greens or a pile of roasted root vegetables? The two starter dressings in this chapter await a spot in your rotation. As does the Herby Fried Shallot and Bread Crumb Crunch (page 234), savory sprinkles that can add texture and oomph to dishes like the White Beans au Vin (page 151). Once you have a batch on hand, you're well on your way to the Lemony Orzo with Asparagus and Garlic Bread Crumbs (page 172).

Need to add protein to a grain bowl? Here's how to make Roasted Chickpeas (page 230) and Baked Tofu (page 229), with smart advice in each that will ensure perfection every time. Go ahead, call *your* mom and tell her the trick to crispy tofu: dusting with cornstarch and skipping foil or parchment for direct contact with the pan.

VEGETABLE STOCK
PAGE 224

LENTILS
PAGE 226

BIG POT OF BEANS
PAGE 227

BAKED TOFU
PAGE 229

ROASTED CHICKPEAS
PAGE 230

MISO-SESAME VINAIGRETTE THAT'S GOOD ON ANYTHING
PAGE 232

VEGAN GREEN GODDESS DRESSING
PAGE 233

HERBY FRIED SHALLOT AND BREAD CRUMB CRUNCH
PAGE 234

VEGETABLE STOCK

VEGAN

time about 1 hour

yield about 2 quarts

Vegetable stock doesn't need the whole vegetable drawer to be savory and flavorful; browned onions, garlic and mushrooms achieve that here, boosted by caramelized tomato paste. The other key ingredient is salt, which transforms the liquid from flat to well rounded, so if your stock seems watery, the answer might not be simmering more but rather adding salt. This stock tastes neutral enough to be used in any recipe that calls for vegetable stock, though you can shift its personality with additional ingredients; see Tip for some ideas.

—Ali Slagle

2 tablespoons extra-virgin olive oil

2 yellow onions, unpeeled, quartered through the root

1 head garlic, unpeeled, halved crosswise

4 to 6 ounces white or brown button mushrooms, stems left on, torn into big pieces

1 tablespoon tomato paste (preferably double-concentrated)

Optional additions (see Tip)

Salt

1. In a large Dutch oven or heavy pot, heat the oil over medium heat. Add the onions and garlic cut sides down and cook until browned, 3 to 5 minutes. Add the mushrooms and cook, stirring often, until the mushrooms are juicy and browned in spots, 3 to 5 minutes. Add the tomato paste and stir constantly until it starts to stick to the pot, 1 to 2 minutes.
2. Add 10 cups (2½ quarts) water, any optional additions and a big pinch of salt. Bring to a boil over medium-high heat. Scrape the browned bits off the bottom of the pot, then reduce heat and simmer gently for 25 minutes.
3. Taste the stock: If it's watery, add a pinch of salt and taste again. If it's still flavorless, keep simmering. Repeat this every 5 minutes or so until the stock is flavorful, which could take anywhere from 25 to 40 minutes total. (If you find the stock bitter or salty, add water to dilute.)
4. Let cool slightly, then strain through a fine-mesh sieve. Refrigerate in an airtight container for up to 1 week or freeze for up to 3 months.

Tip

Add up to 4 cups chopped vegetables, including but not limited to leeks, scallions, celery, celery root, tomatoes, fennel, parsnips, corn and carrots. Be sure to add their stems, leaves and roots, too. (Avoid brassicas and squashes, which can turn the stock bitter and cloudy.) Additional umami boosters include soy sauce, kombu, dried mushrooms, Parmesan rinds, vegetable bouillon and nutritional yeast. You can also add more seasonings, such as fresh thyme, parsley or sage; dried or fresh bay leaves; coriander or fennel seeds; peppercorns; ginger; and fresh or dried chiles.

"I like to do veg stock in the crockpot on low overnight, rather than on the stovetop for an hour. It really improves the depth of flavor."

—Rose

LENTILS

VEGAN

time up to 35 minutes

yield 2 cups

Gentle and creamy lentils add heartiness to soups, salads, sides and so much more. This go-to method works with whole brown, green or black varieties and results in evenly cooked and seasoned lentils. Drained and cooled lentils can be refrigerated in an airtight container for up to 5 days. To freeze, spread the lentils out in a thin layer on a sheet pan or plate and freeze until firm, then transfer to a freezer bag and freeze for up to 3 months.

—Ali Slagle

1 cup whole brown, green or black lentils, picked through and rinsed

Salt

1. Place the lentils in a medium saucepan and add enough water to cover by 1½ inches. Add a big pinch of salt. Bring to a rapid simmer over medium-high heat, then reduce heat to maintain a gentle simmer of slow bubbles. Cook until tender but not mushy, 10 to 30 minutes depending on type and age of lentils. Try one: It should have the texture of al dente pasta, mostly soft but with a little bite in the center.
2. Drain, rinse under cool water to remove exterior starch and shake off excess liquid before eating or storing.

BIG POT OF BEANS

VEGAN

time 1 to 4 hours, plus optional soaking

yield 6 to 8 servings

Chances are good you have some dried beans on hand, and that is a great thing. Especially since one basic recipe works for so many kinds, from red beans to white cannellini to black turtle beans. Choose whichever you like, but bear in mind: Sometimes the best bean is the one already in your pantry.

—Melissa Clark

1 pound any dried beans, rinsed and picked through

Salt

Olive oil, as needed

Aromatics, such as garlic cloves, a halved onion or shallots, a celery stalk or a carrot

Dried or fresh herbs, such as thyme, sage, oregano or rosemary, or a bay leaf or two

A Parmesan rind (optional)

Chopped fresh herbs or celery leaves, sliced scallions or red onion, red pepper flakes, flaky sea salt, for serving (optional)

1. In a large bowl, soak the beans in salted water (it should taste like the sea) for anywhere from 4 to 12 hours. If you don't have time, you can skip this step.
2. Drain the beans and put them in a large pot or electric pressure cooker. If cooking in a regular pot, add enough water to cover the beans by 2 to 3 inches. If using a pressure cooker, use less water, more like 1½ to 2 inches. Add a drizzle of oil and whatever aromatics and herbs you like. Add enough salt to the cooking water to make it taste like the sea.
3. If using a regular pot, simmer the beans for 30 minutes to 2 to 3 hours, depending on what variety you used, how old they were and whether or not you soaked them. Check on them periodically, adding more water if the level gets too low (there should always be enough water to cover the beans). For the pressure cooker, the timing is anywhere from 5 minutes to 50 minutes at high pressure. Let the pressure release naturally.
4. Garnish with fresh herbs or celery leaves, scallions, a drizzle of oil, and a sprinkle of red pepper flakes and flaky sea salt, if using.

"This is the only way I cook tofu. It's so easy and comes out perfectly every time."

—RC

BAKED TOFU

VEGAN

time 50 minutes

yield 2 to 4 servings

This recipe delivers crispy baked tofu that's perfect for salads, stir-fries, curries or rice bowls. Both firm and extra-firm tofu work well, though extra-firm has more bite. Since tofu quality varies significantly among brands, try a few to find your favorite. Skip lining the sheet pan here: Direct contact with the metal pan creates more crispiness. For a shortcut, freeze your tofu first and skip the pressing step entirely.

—Kristina Felix

1 (14- to 16-ounce) block firm or extra-firm tofu, drained

2 tablespoons tamari or reduced-sodium soy sauce

1 tablespoon vegetable oil, plus more for baking sheet

½ teaspoon garlic powder

½ teaspoon onion powder

2 tablespoons cornstarch

1. Place a rack in the center of the oven and heat the oven to 400 degrees.
2. To remove the excess moisture from the tofu, place it between two clean kitchen towels or paper towels, set it on a cooling rack or cutting board in the sink, and place a flat, heavy object, such as another heavy cutting board, a cast-iron skillet or both, on top. Allow the tofu to drain for at least 10 minutes.
3. In a medium bowl, combine the tamari, oil, garlic powder and onion powder and whisk to combine. Cut the pressed tofu into equal-size pieces (¾- to 1-inch cubes). Add the tofu to the bowl with the tamari mixture and toss, making sure the tofu is evenly coated. Sprinkle the cornstarch over and toss until the cornstarch is no longer powdery and adheres to the tofu.
4. Lightly oil a baking sheet and arrange the tofu pieces in a single layer. Bake for 25 to 30 minutes, flipping halfway through with a thin metal spatula, until browned and crispy at the edges. Let cool for about 3 minutes before biting into them, as they will be very hot. Use immediately or let cool completely and store in an airtight container in the fridge for up to 5 days.

ROASTED CHICKPEAS

VEGAN

time 45 minutes

yield About 2 cups

Roasted chickpeas are a pleasantly crisp-on-the-outside, slightly chewy-on-the-inside addition to salads, noodles, soups and grain bowls. Rub the chickpeas vigorously in a dish towel not once but twice to ensure that they're completely dry before sliding them into the oven, and do your best to pick out all the skins that fall off in the process. While this may seem fussy, it's the secret to achieving the crispiest results. To make these chickpeas your own, rummage your spice cabinet and swap the smoked paprika for za'atar, chili powder, garam masala, herbes de Provence or anything else that sounds good.

—Sheela Prakash

2 (15-ounce) cans chickpeas, drained and rinsed (about 3 cups)

2 tablespoons extra-virgin olive oil

Salt

2 teaspoons smoked paprika

1. Heat the oven to 400 degrees. Spread the chickpeas out onto a clean dish towel and rub them thoroughly dry. Discard any skins that happen to fall off in the process. Transfer the chickpeas to another clean dish towel and repeat the process to get them very dry. (The drier the chickpeas, the more success you'll have with crisping them in the oven.)
2. Transfer the chickpeas to a rimmed baking sheet. Drizzle with oil and season generously with salt. Toss well to evenly coat.
3. Roast, shaking the pan every 10 minutes or so, until the chickpeas are golden-brown in spots and crisp, 30 to 35 minutes. Turn off the oven; remove the pan. Immediately sprinkle the chickpeas with the smoked paprika and shake the pan to coat. Taste and season with additional salt as needed. Return the chickpeas to the oven with the door ajar and let them cool and continue to crisp.

Tip

Roasted chickpeas are best served fresh, but leftovers can be stored in an airtight container for up to 1 week. Leave the lid ajar to allow moisture to escape and to keep the chickpeas crisp for longer. If they become chewy, re-crisp on a baking sheet at 400 degrees for about 5 minutes.

"One of my favorite things since I first read about it—has replaced popcorn for movie snacking at home."

—Andy

MISO-SESAME VINAIGRETTE THAT'S GOOD ON ANYTHING

VEGAN

time 5 minutes

yield 1 cup

This all-purpose vinaigrette is great on a simple salad with lettuces and fresh vegetables, such as cucumbers, tomatoes, sliced onions, radishes, jicama or grated carrots. Try it drizzled on an iceberg wedge or over sliced tofu, served hot or cold. It's especially good with spicy greens like watercress, mizuna or arugula.

—J. Kenji López-Alt

2 garlic cloves, smashed with the side of a knife

1 shallot, roughly chopped

2 tablespoons shoyu or tamari

2 tablespoons balsamic vinegar

2 tablespoons red or white wine vinegar

1 tablespoon white miso paste

1 tablespoon dark brown sugar

½ cup grapeseed, vegetable or canola oil

2 tablespoons toasted sesame oil

2 tablespoons toasted white or black sesame seeds

1. In a blender, combine the garlic, shallot, shoyu, vinegars, miso and brown sugar and blend on high speed until homogeneous. (Alternatively, in the bowl of a large mortar, use a pestle to mash the garlic and shallot into a fine paste, then stir in the shoyu, vinegars, miso and sugar.)
2. With the blender running on medium speed (the liquid should form a vortex but not jump up and splatter on the walls of the blender), slowly drizzle in the grapeseed oil. (If using a mortar and pestle, slowly drizzle in the oil as you stir vigorously with the pestle.)
3. Transfer to a lidded jar. Stir in the sesame oil and sesame seeds with a spoon. Dressing can be stored in the fridge for up to 3 weeks. Shake well before using.

VEGAN GREEN GODDESS DRESSING

VEGAN

time 10 minutes

yield 2¼ cups

This creamy, protein-packed dressing uses silken tofu as its base, offering a vegan alternative to the buttermilk or mayonnaise commonly used in more traditional green goddess dressing. The dressing's velvety texture pairs perfectly with crisp winter greens and vegetables such as romaine hearts, Little Gems, radishes, endives and celery. For a satisfying vegetarian meal, consider drizzling it over a hearty bowl with shredded lettuce, cooked grains, legumes and sliced avocado.

—Sue Li

8 ounces silken tofu, drained

4 ounces cilantro stems and leaves (about 1 medium bunch)

2 ounces chives (1 to 2 bunches)

¼ cup fresh lemon juice (from 2 lemons)

1 small jalapeño, quartered (seeds and ribs removed for less heat, if desired)

1 garlic clove

2 teaspoons kosher salt, such as Diamond Crystal

1½ teaspoons sugar

½ teaspoon ground cumin

1. Combine all of the ingredients in a blender along with ¼ cup water and blend until smooth.
2. Store the dressing in an airtight container in the refrigerator for up to 3 days. (The blended tofu might separate a little after it sits, but just stir it to combine before using.)

HERBY FRIED SHALLOT AND BREAD CRUMB CRUNCH

VEGAN

time 45 minutes

yield About 3 cups

This recipe begins with shallots fried Southeast Asian–style, starting in cold oil, using a method so simple you'll never do it any other way. You don't need a thermometer or any other special equipment—just patience and a careful eye. In exchange, you're rewarded with caramel-sweet shallots that crunch then melt between your teeth. Next, rosemary, sage and stale bread crumbs take turns in the oil, crisping as they cool. Then, they're tossed with chopped parsley, thyme and a little flaky salt. From the moment the mixture is done, you won't be able to stop eating it. But if you wait, it makes the perfect topping for green bean casserole, potato gratin, or macaroni and cheese. Sprinkle it atop salads, pastas, casseroles or roasted vegetables, or just put a bowl of it on the table and let people do with it what they will—they'll probably end up putting some on every bite.

—Samin Nosrat

½ large loaf stale country bread, crusts removed, cut into 1-inch cubes (about 5 heaping cups)

2½ cups thinly sliced shallot rings (from about 7 shallots)

2 cups neutral oil, such as canola or safflower oil

Flaky sea salt

12 sage leaves (from 2 to 3 sprigs)

¼ packed cup rosemary leaves (from 4 to 5 sprigs)

3 tablespoons finely chopped flat-leaf parsley leaves (from about ⅓ large bunch)

1 tablespoon finely chopped thyme (from 8 to 9 sprigs)

1. In a food processor, pulse the bread until no pieces larger than a pea remain. Set aside.
2. Line two baking sheets with paper towels and set a fine-mesh sieve over a medium saucepan. Set aside.
3. In a second medium saucepan or a wok, cook the shallots and oil over medium-high heat, stirring frequently, until shallots begin to bubble, about 2 minutes, then reduce heat to medium-low. With the shallots bubbling constantly—the constant bubble is key—continue to fry, stirring regularly to ensure even cooking, until pale golden brown, 24 to 28 minutes longer.
4. Quickly and carefully pour the shallots and the oil into the prepared sieve, draining the oil into the first saucepan. (The shallots will continue to brown and crisp as they cool.) Carefully spread out the shallots on one of the prepared baking sheets and season lightly with flaky salt. Let cool.

Tips

To make ahead, fry shallots, rosemary, sage and bread crumbs up to 1 day in advance. Do not season with salt. Store separately in airtight containers once completely cooled. Just before using, combine the ingredients and add the parsley, thyme and flaky salt.

You can change up the herb combinations or add dried chiles or nuts depending on the time of year. This recipe is endlessly adaptable and will add excitement and crunch to all kinds of dishes, whether soups or pasta, eggs or braises.

5. Reset the sieve over the now-empty second saucepan and set aside. Place the saucepan with the strained oil over medium-high heat and add a sage leaf to test the temperature. (Alternatively, use a thermometer to check that the oil is at 360 degrees.) When the sage leaf sizzles, add remaining sage and the rosemary and stir with a slotted spoon or spider. As soon as the bubbles subside, after 20 to 30 seconds, remove the herbs from the oil and spread them out on the second baking sheet.
6. Add the bread crumbs to the hot oil and stir. Cook, stirring constantly, until golden brown, 3 to 4 minutes, then quickly and carefully pour the bread crumbs and oil into the prepared sieve. Spread bread crumbs on the baking sheet beside the rosemary and sage. Season the herbs and bread crumbs lightly with flaky salt. Let cool.
7. To assemble, in a large bowl, crumble the fried herbs and toss together with the shallots, bread crumbs, parsley, thyme and ¾ teaspoon flaky salt. Taste and adjust seasoning as needed. Store in an airtight container in the fridge for up to 3 days.

ACKNOWLEDGMENTS

I owe a colossal thank-you to the entire NYT Cooking team, who every day confirm that this really is the dream job I thought it was. Thank you to Emily Weinstein, our tremendous editor in chief, for trusting me with the keys to a castle in her illustrious kingdom. I'm forever grateful for the opportunities you continue to afford me. To my work mother, Krysten Chambrot, you are the best boss I've ever had. Thank you for always championing (and putting up with) me. May everyone be so lucky. I am so thankful for Mia Leimkuhler, my newsletter editor, and her unwavering partnership week after week. You make *The Veggie,* and me, sharper for it. I'm sorry this week's newsletter is late. Thank you to Tejal Rao and Mark Josephson, my earliest partners on this Veggie enterprise, to Alexa Weibel, my most trusted vegetarian adviser, to Genevieve Ko, Margaux Laskey, Cathy Lo and Adina Steiman, our formidable recipe editors, and to David Look, of course. And thank you to Sam Sifton for your vision, your wit and your mentorship.

I am graciously indebted to Trish Daly, this book's deft and (and deadline-forgiving) editor, and Caitlin Roper, its fairy godmother and greatest cheerleader. Thank you both for your guidance, your generosity and the gift that is my very own cookbook.

An immense thanks to the team that made it all happen: Erik Borenstein and Debbie Beshaw-Farrell at *The New York Times;* Molly Birnbaum, Laine Whittier, Annie Marino and Stephanie Davis at Ten Speed Press; and Kari Stuart and Christina Darby. And to our most talented art team—Kim Gougenheim, Cat Baldwin, Kate Sears, Monica Pierini, Megan Hedgepeth and Debra Bishop—everything you touch turns to gold (or, in this case, green).

This book would be a spine and a few errant one-liners without the talented recipe developers whose work graces the majority of its pages. Thank you for making me—and millions of readers—better, more inspired cooks. And to the Cooking community and the kind, curious and faithful readers of *The Veggie,* your appetite keeps me going.

To my parents, Andrew and Teresa. I may write for money, but words will always fail to faithfully express my gratitude for what you've given me. Thank you for your support, your patience and your killer taste. You are the blueprint. And to my brother, Alex, who thinks what I do is "awesome." We're not stopping.

Finally, thank you to my confidants, my muses, my special guys: Pippa Allen, Luke Fortney, Becky Hughes, Emily Johnson, Scaachi Koul, Elissa Lynch, Meg Ruocco and Gabe Vasquez. I know I'll never eat alone.

INDEX

A
Afghan-style eggplant in yogurt, 209
asaro (yam and plantain curry), 118–19
asparagus
goat cheese and tarragon tart, 214–15
lemony orzo with, and garlic bread crumbs, 172
white lasagna, 216, 218
avocado
green shakshuka with, and lime, 31
pico de gallo, 86

B
basil tofu, 138
beans and legumes. *See also* chickpea(s); white bean(s)
big pot of beans, 227
brown butter lentil and sweet potato salad, 54–55
coconut black bean soup, 131
creamy, spicy tomato beans and greens, 162
crispy rice with dill and runny eggs, 179
everyday dal, 45
huevos enfrijolados (eggs in spicy black beans), 20
Indian-ish nachos with cheddar, black beans and chutney, 82–83
lentils, 226
no-cook chili bean salad, 52
orzo salad with lentil and zucchini, 74
red lentil soup, 113
vegetarian shepherd's pie, 212–13
white bean, rice and dill soup, 127
béchamel sauce, 216, 218
big pot of beans, 227
biryani, one-pot vegetable, 206–7
bok choy, in somen noodle soup with mushrooms, 128
borani banjan (Afghan-style eggplant in yogurt), 209
Bourguignon, mushroom, 196–97
breakfast tacos, cheesy potato, 42–43
breakfast udon, 24
broccoli
-quinoa soup with turmeric and ginger, 132
quinoa and broccoli spoon salad, 69
brothy Thai curry with silken tofu and herbs, 135
brown butter bucatini with charred cabbage, 165
brown butter lentil and sweet potato salad, 54–55
brown butter, crisp gnocchi with brussels sprouts and, 187
bucatini with charred cabbage, brown butter, 165
buffalo white beans, 94
burritos, roasted vegetable, 81
butternut squash and green curry soup, 124–25

C
cabbage
and Parmesan soup, 110
brown butter bucatini with charred cabbage, 165
cheesy cabbage tteokbokki, 184
parm, 142
cacio e pepe, vegan, 171
Caesar salad, vegan, with crisp chickpeas, 57
carrot(s)
lemony carrot and cauliflower soup, 114
risotto with chile crisp, 168–69
cashew butter, in vegan cacio e pepe, 171
cauliflower
lemony carrot and cauliflower soup, 114
salad sandwiches, 90–91
shawarma with spicy tahini, 78–79
soup with rosemary olive oil, creamy, 106–7
sweet and sour, 154–55
chana masala, 176
cheddar cheese
cheesy cabbage tteokbokki, 184
Indian-ish nachos with cheddar, black beans and chutney, 82–83
pimento cheese and tomato sandwiches, 99
cheese. *See also specific cheeses*
cheesy cabbage tteokbokki, 184
cheesy potato breakfast tacos, 42–43
chhonk, 82–83
chickpea(s)
chana masala, 176
chickpea, spinach and feta pie, 202–3
coconut curry, with pumpkin and lime, 183
miso eggplant salad with, 62
picadillo, 141
roasted, 230
salad sandwiches, 93
vegan Caesar salad with crisp chickpeas, 57
whole roasted squash with tomato-ginger chickpeas, 210–11
chile crisp
carrot risotto with, 168–69
dumplings with, 200–201
vinaigrette, 48–49
chili
in vegetarian tamale pie, 152–53
vegetarian skillet chili, 180
chili bean salad, no-cook, 52
chopped salad
quinoa and broccoli spoon salad, 69
with jalapeño-ranch dressing, 66–67
chutney, cilantro, 82
coconut
black bean soup, 131
crispy coconut rice with tofu, 166
curry chickpeas with pumpkin and lime, 183
dressing, creamy, 70
saag, 148–49
cold tofu salad with tomatoes and peaches, 61
corn and miso pasta salad, 65
cornbread, 152–53
cream cheese, in pimento cheese and tomato sandwiches, 99
crispy coconut rice with tofu, 166
crispy mushroom tacos, 86
crispy rice with dill and runny eggs, 179
crunch, herby fried shallot and bread crumb, 234–35
crunchy veggie wraps with kabocha squash, 85
cucumbers, spicy, with yogurt, lemon and herbs, 73
curried dishes, 10
butternut squash and green curry soup, 124–25
cauliflower salad sandwiches, 90–91
coconut curry chickpeas with pumpkin and lime, 183
crispy coconut rice with tofu, 166
Thai curry with silken tofu and herbs, brothy, 135
yam and plantain curry, 118–19

D
dal, everyday, 45
dill
crispy rice with, and runny eggs, 179
goat cheese and dill Dutch baby, 28
white bean, rice and dill soup, 127
dressing. *See also* vinaigrette
Caesar, 57
creamy coconut, 70
green goddess dressing with silken tofu, vegan, 233
jalapeño-ranch, 66
miso, 62
spicy soy, 188
dumpling(s)
tomato salad with chile crisp vinaigrette, 48–49
with chile crisp, 200–201
Dutch baby, goat cheese and dill, 28

E
egg(s)
cheesy cabbage tteokbokki, 184
crispy rice with dill and runny eggs, 179
eggs in spicy black beans, 20
goat cheese and dill Dutch baby, 28
green shakshuka with avocado and lime, 31
make-ahead egg, spinach and feta wraps, 38–39
more-vegetable-than-egg frittata, 36
eggplant
Afghan-style, in yogurt, 209
Bolognese, 158–59
miso eggplant salad with chickpeas, 62
everyday dal, 45
extra-green pasta salad, 51

F
feta cheese
chickpea, spinach and feta pie, 202–3
make-ahead egg, spinach and feta wraps, 38–39
frittata
herb and scallion, 204–5
more-vegetable-than-egg, 36

G
ginger
broccoli-quinoa soup with turmeric and, 132
vegan salted maple ginger pie, 219–20
gnocchi, crisp, with brussels sprouts and brown butter, 187
goat cheese
and dill Dutch baby, 28

goat cheese, continued
asparagus, goat cheese and tarragon tart, 214–15
gochujang potato stew, 120
grains. *See* quinoa; rice
green goddess dressing with silken tofu, vegan, 233
green shakshuka with avocado and lime, 31
green smoothie, 27
greens. *See also* bok choy; kale; spinach; swiss chard
asaro, 118–19
coconut saag, 148–49
creamed greens potpie, 198–99
creamy, spicy tomato beans and, 162
dumplings with chile crisp, 200–201
golden potato and greens soup, 109
green smoothie, 27
white lasagna, 216
grilled mushroom skewers in red chile paste, 96–97

H
hash, sweet potato, with tofu, 23
herb and scallion frittata, 204–5
herby fried shallot and bread crumb crunch, 234–35
huevos enfrijolados (eggs in spicy black beans), 20

I
Indian-ish nachos with cheddar, black beans and chutney, 82–83

J
jalapeño-ranch dressing, chopped salad with, 66

K
kale
gochujang potato stew, 120
golden potato and greens soup, 109
green smoothie, 27
spring minestrone with, and pasta, 123
vegan Caesar salad with crisp chickpeas, 57
kuku sabzi (herb and scallion frittata), 204–5
kung pao tofu, 144–45

L
laab, mushroom, 157
lasagna, white, 216–18
lemon(y)
carrot and cauliflower soup, 114
orzo with asparagus and garlic bread crumbs, 172
pearl barley soup, 117
ricotta pancakes, 41
lentil(s)
brown butter lentil and sweet potato salad, 54–55
everyday dal, 45
orzo salad with, and zucchini, 74
recipe for, 226
red lentil soup, 113
vegetarian shepherd's pie, 212–13
lime
curry chickpeas with pumpkin and, 183
green shakshuka with avocado and, 31

M
make-ahead egg, spinach and feta wraps, 38–39
maple ginger pie, vegan salted, 219–20
minestrone with kale and pasta, spring, 123
miso
-sesame vinaigrette that's good on anything, 232
corn and miso pasta salad, 65
eggplant salad with chickpeas, 62
more-vegetable-than-egg frittata, 36
mozzarella
cabbage parm, 142
cheesy cabbage tteokbokki, 184
muffins, zucchini, with cinnamon crunch topping, 32–33
mushroom(s)
Bourguignon, 196–97
eggplant Bolognese, 158–59
laab, 157
porcini ragù, 175
portobello au poivre, 147
roasted vegetable burritos, 81
skewers in red chile paste, grilled, 96–97
somen noodle soup with, 128
tacos, crispy, 86
vegetable stock, 224
Wellington, vegetarian, 192–95

N
nachos, Indian-ish, with cheddar, black beans and chutney, 82–83
Nashville-style hot tofu sliders, 102–3
no-cook chili bean salad, 52
noodles
breakfast udon, 24–25
somen noodle soup with mushrooms, 128

O
one-pot vegetable biryani, 206–7
onions, pickled, 180
orzo
lemony, with asparagus and garlic bread crumbs, 172
salad with lentils and zucchini, 74

P
pancakes, lemon ricotta, 41
parm, cabbage, 142
Parmesan, 11
cabbage and Parmesan soup, 110
salad pizza with white beans and, 58
pasta
brown butter bucatini with charred cabbage, 165
cacio e pepe, vegan, 171
eggplant Bolognese, 158–59
lemony orzo with asparagus and garlic bread crumbs, 172
porcini ragù, 175
salad, corn and miso, 65
salad, extra-green, 51
spring minestrone with kale and, 123
white lasagna, 216–18
peaches, cold tofu salad with tomatoes and, 61
pearl barley soup, lemony, 117
picadillo, chickpea, 141
pie
asparagus, goat cheese and tarragon tart, 214–15
chickpea, spinach and feta, 202–3
creamed greens potpie, 198–99
salad pizza with white beans and Parmesan, 58
vegan salted maple ginger, 219–20
vegetarian shepherd's, 212–13
vegetarian tamale, 152–53
pimento cheese and tomato sandwiches, 99
pineapple and jalapeño salsa, 100
pizza
salad pizza with white beans and Parmesan, 58
plantain curry, yam and, 118–19
porcini ragù, 175
portobello au poivre, 147
potatoes
cheesy potato breakfast tacos, 42–43
gochujang potato stew, 120
golden potato and greens soup, 109
vegetarian shepherd's pie, 212–13
potpie, creamed greens, 198–99
pumpkin
coconut curry chickpeas with, and lime, 183

Q
quinoa
and broccoli spoon salad, 69
broccoli-quinoa soup with turmeric and ginger, 132

R
ragù, porcini, 175
red chile paste, grilled mushroom skewers in, 96–97
red lentil(s). *See also* lentil(s)
everyday dal, 45
soup, 113
Reuben sandwich, vegetarian, 89
rice
carrot risotto with chile crisp, 168–69
crispy coconut rice with tofu, 166
crispy rice with dill and runny eggs, 179
one-pot vegetable biryani, 206–7
white bean, rice and dill soup, 127
rice cakes, in cheesy cabbage tteokbokki, 184
ricotta cheese
lemon ricotta pancakes, 41
white lasagna, 216–18
risotto, carrot, with chile crisp, 168–69
roasted chickpeas, 230
roasted vegetable burritos, 81
roasted vegetables with creamy coconut dressing, 70
rosemary olive oil, 106

S
salad
brown butter lentil and sweet potato, 54–55
Caesar salad, vegan, with crisp chickpeas, 57
cauliflower salad sandwiches, 90–91
chickpea salad sandwiches, 93
chopped, with jalapeño-ranch dressing, 66–67
cold tofu, with tomatoes and peaches, 61
dumpling tomato, with chile crisp vinaigrette, 48–49
miso eggplant, with chickpeas, 62
no-cook chili bean, 52
orzo, with lentils and zucchini, 74
pasta salad, corn and miso, 65
pasta salad, extra-green, 51
quinoa and broccoli spoon salad, 69
roasted vegetables with creamy coconut dressing, 70
spicy cucumbers with yogurt, lemon and herbs, 73
salad pizza with white beans and Parmesan, 58
salsa, pineapple and jalapeño, 100
sandwiches. *See also* shawarma; sliders; wraps
cauliflower salad, 90–91
chickpea salad, 93
pimento cheese and tomato, 99
vegetarian Reuben, 89
sauce(s)
avocado pico de gallo, 86
béchamel, 216, 218
chhonk, 82–83
pineapple and jalapeño salsa, 100
spicy tahini, 78–79
sweet and sour, 154–56
scallion and herb frittata, 204–5
scramble, tofu, 35
sesame-miso vinaigrette that's good on anything, 232
shallot and bread crumb crunch, herby fried, 234–35
shawarma, cauliflower, with spicy tahini, 78–79
shepherd's pie, vegetarian, 212–13

shoyu broth, in breakfast udon, 24–25
silken tofu with spicy soy dressing, 188
skillet chili, vegetarian, 180
sliders, Nashville-style hot tofu, 102–3
smoothie, green, 27
somen noodle soup with mushrooms, 128
soup. *See also* stew(s)
broccoli-quinoa, with turmeric and ginger, 132
butternut squash and green curry, 124–25
cabbage and Parmesan, 110
cauliflower, with rosemary olive oil, creamy, 106–7
coconut black bean, 131
golden potato and greens, 109
lemony carrot and cauliflower, 114
lemony pearl barley, 117
red lentil, 113
somen noodle, with mushrooms, 128
spring minestrone with kale and pasta, 123
white bean, rice and dill, 127
spicy cucumbers with yogurt, lemon and herbs, 73
spicy soy dressing, 188
spinach
breakfast udon, 24–25
chickpea, spinach and feta pie, 202–3
extra-green pasta salad, 51
green smoothie, 27
lemony pearl barley soup, 117
make-ahead egg, spinach and feta wraps, 38–39
white lasagna, 216–18
spring minestrone with kale and pasta, 123
squash
butternut, and green curry soup, 124–25
crunchy veggie wraps with kabocha squash, 85
whole roasted, with tomato-ginger chickpeas, 210–11
stew(s)
asaro (yam and plantain curry), 118–19
gochujang potato, 120
mushroom Bourguignon, 196–97
sweet and sour cauliflower, 154–55
sweet potato(es). *See also* yam and plantain curry
brown butter lentil and sweet potato salad, 54–55
roasted vegetable burritos, 81
sweet potato hash with tofu, 23
swiss chard, in green shakshuka with avocado and lime, 31

T

tacos
al pastor, vegan, 100
cheesy potato breakfast, 42–43
crispy mushroom, 86
tahini, cauliflower shawarma with spicy, 78–79
tamale pie, vegetarian, 152–53
tart, asparagus, goat cheese and tarragon, 214–15
tempeh, in vegan tacos al pastor, 100
Thai curry with silken tofu and herbs, brothy, 135
tofu, 10, 11
baked, 229
basil tofu, 138
coconut saag, 148–49
cold tofu salad with tomatoes and peaches, 61
crispy coconut rice with, 166
dumplings with chile crisp, 200–201
kung pao tofu, 144–45
Nashville-style hot tofu sliders, 102–3
scramble, 35
silken, with spicy soy dressing, 188
sweet potato hash with, 23
Thai curry with silken tofu and herbs, brothy, 135
vegan green goddess dressing with silken tofu, 233
vegan salted maple ginger pie, 219–20
tomatoes
chana masala, 176
cold tofu salad with, and peaches, 61
creamy, spicy tomato beans and greens, 162
dumpling tomato salad with chile crisp vinaigrette, 48–49
no-cook chili bean salad, 52
pimento cheese and tomato sandwiches, 99
vegetarian skillet chili, 180
whole roasted squash with tomato-ginger chickpeas, 210–11
toppings
cinnamon crunch, 32–33
herby fried shallot and bread crumb crunch, 234–35
tteokbokki, cheesy cabbage, 184
turmeric and ginger, broccoli-quinoa soup with, 132

U

udon, breakfast, 24–25

V

vegan recipes, 12
breakfast
everyday dal, 45
green smoothie, 27
sweet potato hash with tofu, 23
tofu scramble, 35
comfort food
brown butter bucatini with charred cabbage, 151
chana masala, 176
coconut curry chickpeas with pumpkin and lime, 183
crispy coconut rice with tofu, 166
silken tofu with spicy soy dressing, 188
vegan cacio e pepe, 171
essentials
baked tofu, 229
big pot of beans, 227
green goddess dressing with silken tofu, vegan, 233
herby fried shallot and bread crumb crunch, 234–35
lentils, 226
miso-sesame vinaigrette that's good on anything, 232
roasted chickpeas, 230
vegetable stock, 224
finger foods
cauliflower shawarma with spicy tahini, 78–79
crunchy veggie wraps with kabocha squash, 85
grilled mushroom skewers in red chile paste, 96–97
vegan tacos al pastor, 100
go-to dinners
chickpea picadillo, 141
guest-worthy
dumplings with chile crisp, 200–201
vegan salted maple ginger pie, 219–20
salad
cold tofu, with tomatoes and peaches, 61
corn and miso pasta salad, 65
miso eggplant, with chickpeas, 62
orzo, with lentils and zucchini, 74
roasted vegetables with creamy coconut dressing, 70
vegan Caesar, with crisp chickpeas, 57
soups and stews
asaro (yam and plantain curry), 118–19
broccoli-quinoa soup with turmeric and ginger, 132
brothy Thai curry with silken tofu and herbs, 135
butternut squash and green curry soup, 124–25
creamy cauliflower soup with rosemary olive oil, 106–7
gochujang potato stew, 120
lemony pearl barley soup, 117
mushroom Bourguignon, 196–97
red lentil soup, 113
white bean, rice and dill soup, 127
stir-fry
kung pao tofu, 144–45
vegetable(s). *See also specific vegetables*
biryani, one-pot, 206–7
more-vegetable-than-egg frittata, 36
roasted vegetable burritos, 81
roasted, with creamy coconut dressing, 70
stock, 224
vegetarian mushroom Wellington, 192–95
vegetarian Reuben sandwich, 89
vegetarian shepherd's pie, 212–13
vegetarian skillet chili, 180
vegetarian tamale pie, 152–53
veggie wraps, crunchy, with kabocha squash, 85
vinaigrette
brown butter, 54–55
chile crisp, 48–49
miso-sesame, that's good on anything, 232

W

Wellington, vegetarian mushroom, 192–95
white bean(s)
au vin, 151
buffalo, 94
creamy, spicy tomato beans and greens, 162
gochujang potato stew, 120
salad pizza with, and Parmesan, 58
white bean, rice and dill soup, 127
white lasagna, 216–18
wine, in white beans au vin, 151
wraps
crunchy veggie, with kabocha squash, 85
make-ahead egg, spinach and feta, 38–39

Y

yam and plantain curry, 118–19. *See also* sweet potato(es)
yogurt
Afghan-style eggplant in, 209
spicy cucumbers with yogurt, lemon and herbs, 73

Z

zucchini
muffins with cinnamon crunch topping, 32–33
orzo salad with lentils and, 74

TEN SPEED PRESS
An imprint of the Crown Publishing Group
A division of Penguin Random House LLC
1745 Broadway
New York, NY 10019
tenspeed.com
penguinrandomhouse.com

Page 175, Porcini Ragù adapted from *Mezcla* by Ixta Belfrage (Ten Speed Press, 2022).
Page 214, Asparagus, Goat Cheese and Tarragon Tart adapted from *Dinner in French* by Melissa Clark (Clarkson Potter, 2020).

Library of Congress Cataloging-in-Publication Data is on file with the publisher.

Hardcover ISBN 978-0-593-83662-0
Ebook ISBN 978-0-593-8366-37

Acquiring editor: Molly Birnbaum | Production editor: Terry Deal
Editorial assistants: Gabby Ureña Matos and Laine Whittier
Designers: Debra Bishop, Annie Marino, and Carrie Enock
Typeface: NY San Heavy by A2-Type
Cover designer: Debra Bishop
Cover photographer: Kate Sears
Food stylist: Monica Pierini
Prop stylist: Megan Hedgpeth
Copy editor: Jude Grant
Proofreaders: Jonathan Milder, Rachel Holzman
Indexer: Barbara Mortenson

Manufactured in Malaysia

10 9 8 7 6 5 4 3 2 1

First Edition

The authorized representative in the EU for product safety and compliance is Penguin Random House Ireland, Morrison Chambers, 32 Nassau Street, Dublin D02 YH68, Ireland, https://eu-contact.penguin.ie.

PHOTOGRAPHERS
Andrew Purcell, pages 83, 122, 186
Armando Rafael, page 143
Bobbi Lin, pages 75, 126, 185
Bryan Gardner, pages 59, 67, 140, 159, 203, 207
Christopher Simpson, pages 79, 146, 189, 199, 201, 234
Christopher Testani, pages 49, 114, 164, 177, 193, 228, 231
Con Poulos, page 97
Craig Lee, page 37
Dane Tashima, page 167
David Malosh, pages 2–3, 30, 33, 44, 68, 88, 92, 103, 108, 111, 119, 129, 130, 156, 169, 170, 173, 197, 211, 217
Emma Fishman, page 205
Ghazalle Badiozamani, page 21
James Ransom, page 121
Joel Goldberg, page 39
Johnny Miller, pages 50, 72
Joseph De Leo, page 112
Julia Gartland, pages 95, 101, 155, 139, 178, 181
Kate Sears, page 80
Kelly Marshall, pages 13, 29, 71, 134, 145, 149, 163
Kerry Brewer, page 91
Linda Xiao, pages 8, 22, 25, 56, 60, 87, 107, 116, 125, 133, 150, 174
Mark Weinberg, page 225
Meredith Heuer, page 213
Nico Schinco, pages 43, 53, 64, 208
Rachel Vanni, pages 63, 98, 221
Ryan Liebe, pages 26, 34, 40, 84, 153, 182, 215
Yossy Arefi, page 55

FOOD STYLISTS
Barrett Washburne, pages 21, 26, 34, 40, 43, 59, 64, 67, 80, 83, 84, 95, 98, 119, 121, 140, 153, 178, 182, 186, 199, 203, 207, 208
Carrie Purcell, page 122
Erika Joyce, page 167
Eugene Jho, pages 75, 126
Greg Lofts, page 159
Hadas Smirnoff, pages 8, 39, 60, 87
Jerrie-Joy Redman Lloyd, page 97
Judy Kim, page 133
Kaitlin Wayne, page 53
Liza Jernow, page 181
Maggie Ruggiero, page 174
Monica Pierini, pages 22, 25, 56, 107, 112, 116, 150, 221, 225
Rebecca Jurkevich, pages 72, 202
Roscoe Betsill, pages 29, 71, 134
Samantha Seneviratne, pages 13, 50, 63, 101, 139, 145, 149, 155, 163
Simon Andrews, pages 2–3, 30, 44, 49, 68, 79, 88, 91, 92, 103, 108, 111, 114, 125, 129, 130, 143, 146, 156, 164, 169, 170, 173, 177,189, 193, 197, 211, 215, 217, 228, 231
Sue Li, page 185
Vivian Lui, page 33
Yossy Arefi, page 55

PROP STYLISTS
Christina Lane, page 75
Heather Greene, page 174
Maeve Sheridan, page 134
Megan Hedgpeth, pages 26, 40
Paige Hicks, pages 29, 71, 149
Sophia Eleni Pappas, pages 185, 205